Inner
Happiness

VERA PEIFFER

Inner Happiness

positive steps TO feeling complete

piatkus

PIATKUS

First published in Great Britain in 2002 by Judy Piatkus
(Publishers) Limited
This paperback edition published in 2009 by Piatkus

A CIP catalogue record for this book
is available from the British Library

ISBN 978-0-7499-4141-3

Edited by Catherine Blake
Illustrations by Rodney Paull

Typeset by Action Publishing Technology, Gloucester
Printed and bound in the UK by
CPI Mackays, Chatham ME5 8TD

Papers used by Piatkus are natural, renewable and recyclable
products sourced from well-managed forests and certified
in accordance with the rules of the Forest Stewardship Council.

Mixed Sources
Product group from well-managed
forests and other controlled sources
www.fsc.org Cert no. SGS-COC-004081
© 1996 Forest Stewardship Council

FSC

Piatkus
An imprint of
Little, Brown Book Group
100 Victoria Embankment
London EC4Y 0DY

An Hachette UK Company
www.hachette.co.uk

www.piatkus.co.uk

Dedicated to Ann Parker,
my wonderful health kinesiology teacher,
with love and thanks.

Contents

Introduction   1

PART ONE **Happiness and Emptiness**

Introduction to Part One   7
1. What makes us complete?   8
   Emotional, mental, physical and spiritual health   9
   The link between body and mind   15
   The concepts of energy and vibration   17
   Personal energy   23
   Universal energy   24
   Ego, Self and Soul – three perspectives   27
   Keeping body and Soul together   30

2. Why do we feel incomplete?   31
   Reasons why we feel disconnected   35
   What happens when we are disconnected   56

PART TWO **Becoming Complete**

Introduction to Part Two   67
3. Clearing up the past   69
   Eliminating negative life patterns   70
   Overcoming a limiting past   80
   Transforming emotions through positive
      thoughtforms   94
   Improving your life by changing your perception   102
   Swapping places   105

4. **Being true to your Self** 108

Interacting positively with the world around you 109

Tuning in to your inner world 117

Tuning in to your emotions 119

Tuning in to your spirit 122

Positive visualisation 125

Healing movements 134

The wisdom of nature 141

About flower essences 147

Rebooting your head – electro-magnetic balance 157

Counteracting geopathic stress 163

Surfing everyday chaos 168

Knowing when you are whole again 173

Further Reading 179

Resources 183

Index 192

Only he who can see the invisible can do the impossible.

Frank L. Gaines

Introduction

When I look back over my life, I feel I have come a long way. In my late teens and early twenties, I went through a very difficult phase, feeling depressed and anxious about everything, being unhappy and making everyone else around me unhappy with temper tantrums and day-long sulks. I was afraid of everything and everyone. Conventional psychotherapy helped me to cope much better with my life, but I needed more than that – I wanted to be happy.

My discovery of positive thinking brought me so much closer to my aim. I used positive visualisations and affirmations to increase my confidence and to overcome my fears, and I did so with great success. I became more active and proactive and truly started to enjoy my life. Later, I started writing books about positive thinking and began to teach my methods to others who wanted to learn how to become happier and more confident.

Teaching is of course a very good way of learning, and very soon I found out that my basic techniques of positive thinking were not enough for some of my clients and course participants, so I had to look for more diverse techniques. All of these are now described in my books.

My work as a psychotherapist and analytical hypnotherapist stretches back more than sixteen years, and I am happy to say that in that time I have been able to help a great many people achieve what I have achieved for myself – inner happiness. All my techniques are tried and tested (with myself as prime guinea pig!), and you will find a considerable number of them in this book. By following them, I hope that you in turn can become happier and more confident.

The interesting thing is that I thought there was no more to it, but I was wrong. The icing on the cake was yet to come. One day, my friend Katharina mentioned that she had started studying health kinesiology, and when she told me more about it, I immediately became interested.

Kinesiology allows you to have a 'conversation' with the body to find out what it needs to heal itself and become well again. Any muscle of a patient's body can be used, and will provide information about where the body is functioning below par. The kinesiologist tests the muscle tone of, say, an arm muscle, by exerting very gentle pressure on it. At the same time, he or she touches an acupuncture point on the patient's body which relates to a particular organ – the liver, for example. If the arm muscle yields to the gentle pressure, the therapist knows that the energy influx into the liver is not functioning optimally. This can then be corrected by touching certain acupuncture points, reconnecting the energy flow so that it can move freely towards that organ once again.

I decided to learn about kinesiology myself, and this has opened new doors. It is amazing how working with the body in this way can not only heal physical illnesses but also help overcome emotional stresses and lows. Many of my clients who come to see me because they are unwell notice that in addition to their physical recovery, their emotions begin to lift and they start feeling happier and more positive within themselves. When this correlation between the body and the emotions became so strikingly apparent, I decided to integrate the body-energy approach with my positive thinking techniques for the first time, and the result is this book.

Inner Happiness is a self-help guide for anyone who feels that they are no longer in touch with themselves. It presents a completely holistic approach to combatting the modern malaise of stress and emptiness by giving you a series of mental and energy techniques that work with your mind, body, emotions and Soul. You will discover your own abilities to heal yourself with positive visualisation and affirmation techniques, healing movements and vibrational medicine. *Positive thought is crucial to any healing process, but the picture can often only be completed by working with the energy of your body as well* – as the following case study shows.

In my practical work, helping clients who suffer from bulimia has always been a particularly lengthy and complex task. They have often gone through anorexia before becoming bulimic, which means binge-eating and then making themselves sick. One of my clients, Alison, a young woman of twenty-four, had gone through just that. We spent considerable time working through issues that concerned her dysfunctional family background with analytical hypnotherapy, but with only limited success. Alison was making herself sick less frequently but seemed unable to stop it altogether. At my suggestion, she agreed to change over to health kinesiology treatment, and by simply balancing her body's meridians in the first session, her bingeing reduced further.

In her fourth session, we discovered that the issue of death was a cause of great stress to her. This was because a year previously she had experimented with 'magic' mushrooms, which are powerful hallucinogens, and had had a very bad experience: she had collapsed and thought she was dying. While she remembered this experience, I held acupuncture points on her to help her body release the stress around this issue. After that fourth session, Alison stopped bingeing altogether, and six months later when I met her in the street, she told me that she was still eating normally.

Past trauma may have left you feeling at the end of your tether, empty, alone and disconnected, not only from your own person, but also from life around you. If you cannot connect with the outside world in a meaningful way, you 'lose' some of your feelings, and this means that you lose part of what makes up your Self.

Inner emptiness separates you from your environment and stops you from bonding with others. The techniques set out here will help you break this vicious circle. Remember that it can affect anyone, even those who do well in life, who are successful and have all the trappings of modern civilisation. You shouldn't feel ashamed if you have been lucky in life, but still feel something is missing.

Our tendency to cocoon ourselves into our home, where we increasingly relate to the outside world through a television or the Internet, is progressively eroding our ability to feel part of the amazing world inside and around us. We are beginning to live in a narrower and narrower corridor of life experiences where we depend on soaps and computer games for our daily high, and where our life is governed by our desire for new products which in the end can only give us temporary satisfaction.

Alcohol and recreational drugs often provide the quick-fix solution to the resulting feelings of inner emptiness. They help us calm down or speed up, they help us forget or cover up what we don't want to face, they make us see weird and wonderful things in our mind – and they isolate us. The trip only lasts so long, and then we are left with emptiness and a feeling of being disconnected from ourselves and from people around us.

Unhappiness and inner emptiness can be covered up in many different ways. The current obsession with endless shopping for new clothes and accessories is one of them. Our urge to buy and acquire much more than we could ever need to wear seems to suggest that we spend a lot of time looking at our outer appearance. Is that because we have no inner life? Or is it because we don't know how to access our inner resources, which can provide us with so much more fulfilment and happiness than consumerism could ever give us? The fact is that if your life revolves only around possessions, it could be that you are no longer in touch with your Self.

In order to be a whole person, we need not only to be in touch with all our emotions, including the unpleasant ones, but also to have the right balance between these feelings, enabling us to interact successfully with our social environment. Our upbringing and past experiences may have taught us to suppress certain feelings or leave others unexpressed, and it can be quite a challenge to readjust them. But it is worth the effort! Balanced emotions give us the space in our minds to develop further and connect with the essence of our being – our Soul. This connection allows us to live in peace and harmony with ourselves and people around us.

Inner Happiness is the first book that offers a fully holistic programme to help you shift your mindset to a positive outlook and enhance your physical energy. It sets out practical solutions to the problems of inner disintegration and emptiness. The techniques in this book will help you break free from body–mind boundaries and discover deeper levels of personal development.

Part 1 examines why we may feel disconnected, empty or incomplete, and explains how this can affect our psychological and physical well-being. I will also be looking at the ingredients you will need to put yourself back together if you feel you have fallen to pieces or if you simply sense that something important is missing from your life. In this area, the concepts of energy and vibration (strange as they may sound!) are an important factor in building up and maintaining health and psychological well-being. Body–mind concepts are clearly explained, as are the forces of energy and vibration, and how they serve your body and mind. These concepts are supported by scientific research which shows that we are indeed more than the sum of our body parts. So please don't skip Part 1 as it is important for your understanding of Part 2!

In Part 2, we look at ways to overcome inner feelings of emptiness and frustration. Here, you will find a wealth of everyday examples, exercises and case studies to help you develop more comprehensive healing and personal growth strategies for yourself. Some of these strategies may be familiar to you, others may feel new and a little strange. All I am asking is that you keep an open mind. The techniques have been tried and tested and will supply you with very useful resources to tackle anything that is stopping you from enjoying your life to the full. Anything new can appear strange, but once you see the results you can't imagine how you could ever have doubted they could work.

PART ONE

Happiness and Emptiness

Introduction to Part One

When we want to overcome an inner sense of emptiness, it is very important to understand what exactly it is that disturbs our inner equilibrium. You may be aware of not being happy in your relationship with your partner, but when a problem has been going on for a long time, you begin to get used to it.

As you are slowly drifting into unhappiness, you can easily begin to believe that this is all there is to life – a mediocre or even unsatisfying relationship that you simply have to learn to put up with. If your best friend were in your situation, you would probably advise them to get out of the relationship, but when you yourself are in the middle of it, it becomes more difficult to see this. The section on the different psychological, physical and environmental causes for inner emptiness will help you to take a step back and recognise your own situation more clearly.

We then go on to look at the effects that these problem situations can have on your psyche. Depression, anxiety, anger and dependency are often caused by psychological problems, but did you know that a food allergy can make you nervous and depressed?

CHAPTER ONE

What makes us complete?

How do we know if we are complete? It is often easier to tell when something is wrong than to know how it should be when it is right. What is involved in being 'whole'?

Being 'complete' or 'whole' means that we are a fully intact human being in a psychological sense. You may go bald or have lost a leg in an accident, but that need not influence your feelings of being complete. Being 'whole' means having self-confidence and generally feeling positive about your person and your life. It also means accepting yourself with all your strengths and faults.

When you feel complete, you enjoy what you have. At the same time, you feel able to change those things in your life that need improvement and accept those things that cannot be changed. You relate with ease to the people with whom you come into contact on an everyday basis. This does not mean that we should have only positive or fulfilling relationships with others. Someone who is a complete person can be at odds with themselves and people around them at times; after all, this is part of growing up, developing as a person and becoming mature. Being at odds with yourself or others need not stop you engaging with the world around you.

In order to feel whole, we need a sense of Self, a sense of who we are, what our values are, and how we relate to others, be they family, colleagues, neighbours or complete strangers.

In addition, we also need to be tuned in to our own feelings, to our body and to nature around us. This means that we have not only to look at the physical, mental and emotional level of existence, but over and above, go one step further and explore the spiritual side of human nature. It is only when all four aspects of life interweave successfully that we are truly complete. So let us now look at all four components – physical, mental, emotional and spiritual – in more detail.

Emotional, mental, physical and spiritual health

Before we go any further, it is important to understand that although we need to be healthy in the four essential areas of life, please don't worry – you don't have to be 100 per cent in all of them to feel whole. Having weaknesses is part of being human. What you do have to have, however, is a sense of harmony and balance in each of these areas. Balance gives you flexibility, and flexibility is crucial, as it allows you to tolerate a fair amount of ups and downs, and to adapt in a more constructive way to life's challenges.

Emotions, body, mind and spirit are of course closely interwoven, but I would first of all like to take a brief look at each area separately to see how balance and harmony can be achieved. I will look at the spiritual side in a little more detail because it is the part of us that is most commonly overlooked and therefore needs most explanation.

Emotional health

As children grow up, they are taught to adapt to the people around them. This means suppressing or at least reining in those emotions that are considered 'negative'. In Western cultures, these include anger, envy, pride and greed. During the socialisation process, the young person learns to fit in with the rest of the community without causing harm to others or standing out for any undesirable reason. The parameters that govern acceptable social behaviour will usually demand that impulsive or antisocial behaviour is ruled out.

The line between being emotionally healthy and being overly adjusted to society's demands can be a narrow one. The best way of describing emotional health is probably the ability to experience the full range of emotions (with the positive ones far outweighing the negative), while relating peacefully to people around you.

Is your emotional health okay?
Give yourself one point for every statement that applies to you.

1. I'm often in a bad mood.
2. I find it difficult to control my anger.
3. I find it hard to say 'no', even when someone makes unreasonable demands.
4. I am a jealous person.
5. I'm easily hurt when I'm criticised, even if the criticism is constructive.
6. It upsets me greatly when I fail at something, no matter how unimportant it is.
7. I feel I'm losing control over my life.
8. I feel anxious and down a lot.
9. I can't let go of a past event.
10. I feel unhappy about lots of things in my life.

0–2 points: Is there an obvious reason why you feel this way? Is there anything you can do to change your situation? If there *is* something you can do, are you doing it? If you are okay on all other counts, you should be able to sort out your emotions by doing the exercises in this book.

3–6 points: There seem to be quite a few problems with your emotions. Work through the exercises, but if you cannot untangle your feelings on your own, seek professional help (see Resources, page 183).

7-10 points: You are on an emotional rollercoaster at the moment. Seek professional help (see Resources, page 183) and use the exercises in this book as additional support to further the healing process.

Mental health

The rational mind is run by the left hemisphere of the brain and helps us with logical tasks such as calculating, arranging, sorting and everyday decision-making. When we decide how to arrange our clothes in the wardrobe, or in which order to carry out our daily tasks, we do so with the help of our rational mind.

Rational thinking is greatly influenced by the state of your emotions. If you are upset or frightened, the rational mind is prevented from working to its full potential. Concentration, recall and decision-making become an impossibility when your feeling levels are in turmoil.

The ability to think in a rational way is important as a counterpoint to our emotions, and allows us to structure our lives with a clear head. A sign of good mental health is the ability to think rationally without making rational thinking into a mechanism whose only function is to suppress the emotions.

Is your rational mind in working order?
Give yourself one point for every statement that applies to you.

1. I'm so emotional that I often find it hard to make rational decisions.

2. I constantly change my mind. I'm a true ditherer.

3. In certain situations, I panic and am unable to think rationally.

4. I find it difficult to follow a train of thought when I need to take in new information.

5. I feel confused and disorientated.

6. I find it difficult to follow instructions. I simply cannot remember the order of things.

The more statements apply to you, the more seriously your rational thinking is compromised. This is usually a consequence of emotional overload. Chances are that if you ticked a lot of the statements in the emotions test, you may have also ticked quite a few in this test. As you are sorting out your emotions, you will notice that your rational thinking will come in line automatically. Bear in mind as well that your rational thinking may be impaired by external factors, including environmental disruption (see pages 51–5).

Physical health

The body is the vehicle that carries our emotions, our mind and our Soul. It is the outer shell that establishes the boundary between us and our environment, but it is also nurtured *by* the environment, via air, light and food. As the state of the body can have an influence on both the rational mind and the emotions, it is important to ensure that the body has all it needs to keep it functioning as smoothly as possible. This means:

- Moderate regular exercise.

- Foods that are varied, natural and nutritious.

- Air to breathe that is as clean as possible.

- A sufficient amount of good-quality water every day to keep the body hydrated.

A healthy body is one that has energy, is free of disease and is therefore strong enough to support us through emotionally stressful periods. It also allows the brain to work efficiently and so make rational thinking much easier.

How good is your physical health?
Give yourself one point for every statement that applies to you.

1. I feel constantly tired.

2. Whenever there is a bug going around, I'll catch it.

3. I have been plagued by various health problems for a long time.

4. I have a chronic condition which doesn't get better.

5. I have a chronic condition which is getting worse.

6. I have annoying physical symptoms (ticks, twitches, shooting pains, and so on) that keep recurring.

7. The quality of my skin and/or hair has deteriorated.

8. My breathing feels different in an unpleasant way.

9. I feel unwell but can't say exactly how or why.

10. One (or several) of my body processes (menstruation, bowel movements, digestion, for example) has not been working properly for a while.

If your score is fairly high, it does not necessarily mean that you are gravely ill. Several of the above can be caused by the same underlying condition.

The best course of action is to see your GP. If they cannot help or won't refer you, consider having a complete health screen with all the necessary tests. If nothing can be found, consider the possibility of environmental disruption in your home or office (see pages 51–5) and have these checked out by an expert (see Resources, page 183). And if all else fails (or better still, *before* all else fails), see a practitioner who works with subtle energies. Many conditions and imbalances that do not show up in conventional medical tests can be diagnosed and healed with subtle energy methods (see page 17).

Spiritual health

So far, we have been looking at the day-to-day aspects of health: the body, mind and emotions. We are familiar with them, we read about them, we speak about them. It is the final part of the whole, however, that tends to get less attention – the inner, or 'spiritual', aspect of each individual. Many people equate spirituality with church, religion or even the occult;

others regard this inner world as an abstract philosophical concept; but it does not have to be abstruse or off-the-wall. You may find it helpful to think of the spiritual side of life as an appreciation of the process of life itself that leads us beyond the purely personal. It doesn't matter if you are not religious; all you need to access your spiritual side is openness and a sense of curiosity.

Spirituality is a very real thing and in many ways quite ordinary. Check whether you have ever done or experienced any of the following:

1. Had your breath taken away by a particularly spectacular view.

2. Looked closely at a plant or flower and marvelled at the intricacy of its design.

3. Felt blissfully happy for a moment in time, without any obvious reason.

4. Felt a very strong affinity with another person without knowing why.

5. Thought about someone you haven't seen in a while only to be contacted by them shortly afterwards.

6. Felt comforted by prayer in times of distress.

7. Felt a special atmosphere in a particular place.

8. Sensed an emotionally charged atmosphere as you joined a group of people.

As you can see, none of the above is at all uncommon, and if any one of them is familiar to you personally, you have had a spiritual experience These experiences are extra-sensory, which means they are a very marked inner feeling that cannot be attributed to any of our 'normal' senses. Spiritual experiences touch the core of our being, and it is this core that I consider to be the human Soul. In order to be happy and feel complete, we need to get in touch with our Soul on a regular basis, as it helps support and nurture all other aspects of our life.

Identifying with this inner world is the key to finding that missing part of our Selves.

All sides of our Selves – physical, mental, emotional and spiritual – are interconnected and need to work harmoniously together for us to experience inner happiness I would like now to look at how we have come to understand the interrelationship of these aspects. Before we explore the concepts of energy and vibration, let us first of all see how the body relates to the mind.

The link between body and mind

As far back as the 1940s, laboratory procedures were developed in the US that trained research subjects to alter normally involuntary bodily functions such as brain activity, blood pressure, muscle tension and heart rate. In the late 1960s, the term 'biofeedback' was coined to describe this training technique, whereby people could be taught to improve their health and performance by using signals from their own bodies. Other biological functions that people have learnt to control with biofeedback are skin temperature and pain (including phantom pain).

In a typical biofeedback session, the trainee is connected up to a device that picks up electrical signals from the muscles and translates these into either a visual or auditory signal on the biofeedback machine. Every time the trainee's muscles tense, the device triggers a flashing light or activates a beeper. The trainee is instructed to find a way, either through thoughts or breathing, to slow down the flashing or beeping. In this way, they learn not only to associate sensations from the muscle with actual levels of tension, but also to use certain thoughts to help muscles relax. An early example of positive thinking!

This is in essence how positive thinking and hypnotherapy work, only without the gadgets. By helping a patient relax the body and focus the mind, a hypnotherapist can help control asthma, speed up healing after operations or accidents, reduce hayfever symptoms, combat stress, and much more. Quite clearly, we have more control over so-called involuntary bodily functions than was once thought possible, and the control mechanism that helps us to achieve this is our mind.

Most people have had personal experience of the mind's influence on the body. You may have had to give a presentation in front of colleagues, but the mere *thought* of it made your stomach turn. You may have dreaded going to the dentist's and found that you were so nervous the night before that your sleep was disrupted. The thought of the coming event triggered a physical reaction, even though it had not yet happened.

The most powerful aspect of thought as a major cause of illness is fear, because anxiety weakens the immune system. An old Arab tale illustrates this point very clearly:

On a desert road, Pestilence met a caravan on its way to Baghdad. 'Why are you going to Baghdad?' asked the Arab in charge of the caravan. 'To take five thousand lives,' replied Pestilence. On the way back from the city, the paths of Pestilence and the caravan crossed once more. 'You told me a lie,' protested the Arab angrily to Pestilence. 'Instead of five thousand lives you took fifty thousand!' 'That is untrue,' replied Pestilence. 'I told you no lie. I said I would take five thousand lives and that is all I took, not one more or less. It was fear that killed the rest.'

It is not just the mind that influences the body – the body also influences the mind. When you have cut yourself, for example, this injury will have an effect on your mind and your emotions. As well as the severity of the wound, it is your personality and cultural background that will decide how you cope. Some personality types are clearly tougher than others and will have a fairly high pain threshold. Not only do these people experience a wound as less painful than a more sensitive person, but they will also be less distressed by the fact that they have been injured. In contrast, children growing up in a culture where injuries are generally commented on with noisy laments and a great deal of fussing will learn that to be physically hurt is extremely upsetting. The child's pain threshold will therefore be low, so that even a small injury is experienced as very painful.

Just as a physical injury can affect our mental state, so can illnesses and allergies. As the body is struggling with the invasion of an unwelcome substance, be it an allergen, a bacterium or a virus, our mood drops and we feel low, disoriented, uncoordinated and indecisive. Illness and allergies can virtually 'disable' us mentally.

The concepts of energy and vibration

In order to arrive at a better understanding of the spiritual component in our lives and how it fits into our overall wellbeing, I would like to introduce you to a concept of health which will probably be new to you.

Current Western allopathic medicine addresses the state of the physical body *only*, and both the cause and the cure of disease are treated as physical. If you suffer from an acute or chronic physical, mental or emotional illness, your doctor will give you tablets that influence the chemical balance of your body to eliminate your symptoms. The fact that a person gets ill in the first place is put down to bacteria, viruses or genetics that predisposed the sufferer to the disorder or the disease.

In Chinese medicine, physical, mental and emotional health is seen as a direct reflection of the state of the underlying energy system, the acupuncture meridians. The meridians are pathways that carry subtle energy, also known as *ch'i*, through the body, just as arteries and veins carry blood through our system. Imbalances in the meridian system are believed to lead to acute and eventually chronic disease.

A disruption in the flow of subtle energy can be caused by an enormous number of different factors: environmental chemicals, poor nutrition, polluted air, detrimental relationships, electro-magnetic disturbances, persistent negative thoughts and emotions, and so on. When the meridian energy system is brought back into balance, the body is able to heal itself. Meridians can be rebalanced through acupuncture, health kinesiology and many other forms of therapy that work with the body's subtle energies.

Meridians – the body's energy motorways

The energy flowing through the meridians is called 'subtle energy' because, up until recently, it has not been possible to measure it with even the most sensitive scientific instruments. In 1985, however, the French researcher Pierre de Vernejoul and his team found that radioactive technetium injected into a patient's acupuncture points travelled along classical Chinese acupuncture meridian pathways through the body. When they injected the substance into random points on the skin, into veins or lymphatic channels, no such distribution occurred.

This suggested that these unique and separate pathways through the body do exist. Subsequent trials on animals showed that when the meridian pathway relating to the liver was severed, the liver began to degenerate after a few days, even though the blood vessels and nerves supplying the liver were unharmed. These studies seem to confirm that the meridians do indeed provide a specialised subtle energy to the organs, without which the organs cannot live.

You may find it helpful to think about the meridians as energy 'motorways' that lead to particular organs and glands, and acupuncture points as the sliproads that allow traffic on to the motorway. For an organ to function, it needs subtle energy from the environment outside. Imagine lorries full of energy entering the sliproads and carrying their load along the meridian motorway to the organ. But what happens if one or several of the sliproads is blocked? The lorries cannot get on to the motorway, so fewer lorries carry energy to the organ. Equally, if roadworks or obstacles stop traffic, there is one big stationary traffic jam and no energy gets through to the organ.

Body, mind and emotions are run by two sensory systems: the nervous system and the electro-magnetic system. The nervous system sends electrical impulses through the body to control the sense organs, the motor functions and all our metabolic processes. The electro-magnetic system, on the other hand, regulates the energies of the vital organs, controls the pituitary and pineal glands, powers the immune system and stimulates healing when it senses injury. It is the electro-magnetic system that operates via the meridians and uses the acupuncture points to draw in energy from the environment in much the same way as we breathe in air.

Let's now have a closer look at how magnetism works as an outside source of subtle energy and how it affects our well-being.

Magnetic forces at work

The Earth is a huge magnet with a north (negative) and a south (positive) pole, with its field covering the whole surface of the planet and exerting its magnetic force on all living beings. There is a *positive* charge below the Earth's crust, a *negative* charge on its surface and a *positive* charge in the upper atmosphere emanating from the Sun's energy. The *negative* magnetic field on the Earth's surface is essential for health and normal evolution.

As a consequence of the Earth's electro-magnetic field, everything within our bodies vibrates, right down to the electrons within every single cell. Wherever there is an electro-magnetic field, there is movement. We know that electricity *flows* – it is a dynamic force. We also know that magnets attract objects with a different polarity but repel others with the same polarity. Again, this is an active phenomenon which involves movement.

Magnetism is the force that keeps order in the galaxy, making stars and planets spin. And just like any other living organism in the world, our bodies are naturally electro-magnetic. That is why modern medicine can use devices and techniques such as electrocardiograms, electroencephalograms and magnetic resonance imaging (MRI) in hospitals to monitor the magnetic fields of the human body and thereby ascertain a patient's state of health. This internal magnetism also helps the circulation of food and oxygen by agitating the cells and increasing their surface area so that nutrients can be absorbed and distributed faster and more efficiently.

Considering the importance of the Earth's magnetic field to our health, it is not surprising that abnormal frequencies from mobile phones and microwaves can be harmful. Looking at human health in subtle energy terms, it becomes immediately clear why there should be a higher incidence of life-threatening diseases such as cancers near power stations or power lines, which disturb the electro-magnetic balance of the meridian pathways, thus blocking the energy 'motorways'.

Other factors that disrupt the smooth flow of energy through the meridians are:

Emotional stress This will result in an imbalance of both the nervous and the electro-magnetic systems and can lead to illness (psychosomatic illness).

Geopathic stress The Earth itself can generate abnormal energy fields. Underground streams as well as naturally occurring Earth energy lines can lead to health problems if houses are built on land where these lines cross.

Chemical toxins These can be noxious fumes and vapours in the air we breathe, or perhaps contained in everyday cleaning agents that we use in the house or at work. Food preservatives, colourings and flavourings can also become a problem to sensitive people, as can amalgam tooth fillings.

Rogue electric currents When we have dissimilar metals in the body such as amalgam fillings in our teeth, electric currents are generated in the mouth which will arc between the metals and disturb our electro-magnetic field.

Mechanical shock or impact It appears that a bad fall or a car crash, for example, can cause subtle energy disturbances. Apart from the accident-related injuries, the subtle energy disturbance can lead to impaired intellectual or physical functioning, even when the physical wounds may have healed.

Scar tissue Scars that run along or cross acupuncture meridians can cause the meridian to become blocked as the flow of subtle energy is disrupted. On a physical level, this manifests as redness, swelling, numbness and sensitivity in that area, and it can also prevent other muscles and organs from functioning fully.

Please don't be concerned if you find you are having problems in any of the above categories. All this can be sorted out and there is a lot you can do to help yourself. Ways to counter-balance energy disturbances and re-establish a healthy flow of energy are explained in Part 2.

Good vibes

Electro-magnetism creates vibration. The word 'vibration' is derived from the Latin *vibrare*, meaning 'to shake' – the motion of an object going back and forth. The number of cycles the motion goes through per unit of time is called the frequency, measured in hertz (Hz). When you are healthy, your body vibrates at about 300 Hz, when you have a fever, your vibrational rate goes up to 475 Hz. This higher frequency generates more energy so your body can fight the invading cold bacteria better.

The human energy field is tuned to the Earth's electro-magnetic field, which pulsates within a range of 1 to 30 Hz. The dominant frequency lies between 7 and 19 Hz, which is exactly the frequency at which the human brain operates under normal conditions.

Researchers at Manchester University discovered that humans have a mass of magnetic crystals slightly in front of the pineal gland that helps us to resonate harmoniously with the Earth's electro-magnetic field. Scientists at NASA found that the absence of this field in space caused astronauts to feel unwell on their return home. They therefore built magnetic field generators into the space shuttles to vibrate at 7.8 Hz, providing the astronauts with the same magnetic environment they would have on Earth. This solved the problem.

It is not only living organisms that are electro-magnetic by nature, but also everything else that shares the Earth with us:

minerals, metals and even man-made objects and substances such as plastic, glass, wooden furniture, paper handkerchiefs, and so on. They all have their own unique vibrational frequencies, also known as *energy patterns*. Virtually every single object around us has its own specific energy pattern.

If an object vibrates at a very low rate, you can see the object; if it vibrates at a very high rate, the object becomes invisible. When you tap a tuning fork, you can *hear* a sound that is caused by the metal prongs making the surrounding air vibrate at a high frequency. This vibration (which we call sound) falls within a frequency range that is no longer accessible to the human eye but can still be registered by our ears. When sound waves are very loud, like those coming from our neighbour's stereo, we can also *feel* the vibration of the air in our whole body, and this can sometimes create a painful physical sensation in the ears.

The same thing is true for the sound of a voice. Depending on *what* you say and *how* you say it, your voice will vibrate at a particular frequency and affect yourself and those listening to you accordingly. Even thoughts and written words have their own unique vibrational quality, which was proved in an amazing scientific experiment conducted in Japan by Dr Masaru Emoto.

Dr Emoto filled a number of identical glass vials with water, and then stuck labels on the vials which had either a positive or a negative word written on them. The vials were then put into a freezer and kept there for a period of time. When he later examined the frozen water under a microscope, Dr Emoto discovered that all the vials with negative words had developed nondescript blobs in the frozen water, whereas all the vials with positive words were showing beautiful ice crystals.

Just as a violinist produces a certain sound by guiding the bow over one particular string, so a word can evoke a particular feeling inside you. You may have noticed when you are reading a book how certain sentences can 'move' you. Sometimes you go over a particular phrase again and again because it makes you feel good. This means that those words vibrate at a frequency that activates your inner feelings of happiness. This is why it is so important to make sure you think and speak positively, as positive thoughts vibrate within you to bring about physical health and emotional well-being.

Personal energy

To be healthy and enjoy life, we need to make sure that our subtle energies can flow freely through our body via the meridian system. Disruption of our subtle energies impacts not only on our physical health but also on our mental, emotional and spiritual state. Like ripples on a pond, its effect spreads to other areas of our lives.

When subtle energy flow is blocked, it can make us feel confused, muddle-headed, unable to concentrate or think logically, indecisive and anxious. When we are anxious, we are more likely to make mistakes. We will therefore be less willing to attempt new things, consequently lack practice in creating success for ourselves and so become even more anxious.

Eventually, this culminates in an emotional withdrawal from people around us, as we don't want them to discover how inefficient, unsuccessful or worthless we are. It is at this point that the vicious circle spins out of control: we start living in our heads and, alone with our own thoughts, we allow them to become a thing in themselves which starts ruling our life. We disappear into ourselves.

Our anxiety and shame about our perceived inadequacies cuts us off from the outside world, when it is this world and its reactions to us that can help us realise that our perception of ourselves does not in fact reflect reality. We now are a prisoner in our own head – we have lost touch with our Self.

There are a number of things we can do now. We can make sure we eat the right foods, eliminate anything from our diet or environment that we are allergic to, hydrate the body by drinking enough water and take moderate exercise to help the cardiovascular and lymph systems work efficiently.

If you feel your present ill health or unhappiness is caused by present or past trauma, it makes sense to seek professional help. Psychotherapy, carried out by a sensitive and competent therapist, is a godsend to many sufferers, and I would recommend it to everyone. But when we feel off-balance, we need to start looking beyond the body–mind link if we want to solve those personal problems that do not respond to conventional psychotherapy or drug treatment.

When we get ill or feel we are withdrawing into ourselves, we need to look at what is preventing the flow of subtle energies through our body systems so we can redress the imbalance. There are many ways in which we can help ourselves heal body and mind and reconnect to the world around us, and you will find a great number of self-help methods in Part 2. But before we go on to look at practical ways of putting your Self back together, let me take you one step further.

Universal energy

I couldn't sleep. Again. This was the third night in a row that I had woken up in the middle of the night. What was the matter? There were no funny noises in the house, I had no particular worries and I wasn't feeling unwell, but I had woken up, which is unusual as I am normally a sound sleeper.

I had a feeling that I needed calcium, without knowing why. It was just a vague thought that seemed to have entered my head from nowhere. I didn't want to turn on the light in case that woke me up even more, so I traipsed over to my treatment room in the dim light coming from a street lamp outside the windows. Calcium. In one of my bookcases, I keep a variety of homeopathic remedies and supplements and I decided just to run my hand over the top of about twenty remedies that were on that top shelf, thinking 'Can I please have the right remedy to help me sleep?'

My hand seemed to gravitate towards a particular container which I picked up and took back to my bedroom. By now I was curious to find out what it was, so I decided to turn on the light after all to read the label. It was Tissue Salt No. 1 – calcium fluoride. I took a dose and slept like a baby.

Weird? Peculiar? Unreal? A lucky dip or just coincidence? At that time, I thought it was amazing; now I think it's normal because similar things have happened so many times that they are no longer unusual. I now know that they are *not* coincidences but that *I make them happen* and that, in effect, everyone can do the same thing with a bit of practice.

So how did I know I needed calcium and how could I find the right remedy in the dark amongst such a great number? I am not particularly gifted, I am not a clairvoyant and I have no hidden talents of divination, and yet, I can pick the right remedy by passing my hand over the containers, and I can test a number of other things – pick the right foods in the super-market, or the right position for my plants in my house, and tell whether food in the fridge is still okay to eat. All I do is touch the item with one hand and do a simple muscle test with the other. Having trained my fingers to give me a 'yes' or 'no' response, I can ask 'Is this the right remedy?' or 'Is this food in the fridge still all right?', and my fingers will tell me 'yes' or 'no'. It is just a matter of practice, and later on in the book, you will learn how to do a little of this muscle testing for yourself.

Through my training as a health kinesiologist, I have learnt to tune into muscle signals that my body gives me when it detects the correct energy pattern that will provide the needed energetic vibration to restore a balanced body frequency. The fact that calcium came to my mind, even before I ran my hand over the tissue salts, just demonstrates an advanced ability to tune into remedy patterns.

I had in the past read the labels on each tissue salt container while I held it in my hand. This gave my body an opportunity to 'learn' the energy pattern of each tissue salt (there are twelve overall) so it could later recognise it as appropriate to the present state of my energy needs. At the same time, reading the label on the tissue salt container locked the individual energy pattern to a name. So when I couldn't sleep, my body knew which energy pattern was needed to redress my body's unbalanced frequency and its name was 'calcium'.

Testing as I have described above enables us to link into the 'bigger picture' of how we relate, not to the people in our environment, but to the *universe* around us, of which we are all part. When we are happy and healthy, with all the subtle energies freely flowing through the meridians, our bodies vibrate at a particular frequency. When we are unwell or unhappy, the frequency is less harmonious. This was the case for me when I could not sleep. Had my body been unable to shift its energetic mode back to normal by itself, I would have been able to go back to sleep. However, my body needed some help – it needed a subtle energy boost.

Tapping into subtle energies through muscle testing or dowsing is a way of connecting us to nature and the universe. This makes sense because, after all, our lives are governed by nature. We are living within the energy field of the Earth's and the Sun's powerful magnetic fields. We are influenced by the Moon, which governs women's menstrual cycle and the oceans' tidal movements.

With the mass of electro-magnetic crystals lodged in front of our pineal gland, we resonate harmoniously to the Earth's electro-magnetic field. Birds migrate using the Earth's magnetic field, and whales are also thought to navigate over great distances with the help of Earth magnetism. The Earth and the surrounding universe have an influence on our health and on our mood. When the air is filled with positive ions just before and during a thunderstorm, many people become anxious and unwell, or develop headaches. This is because their bodies have difficulty adapting to the changed magnetic field of the surrounding atmosphere.

It is this link we have to the Earth and the universe that we need to understand and utilise more in our daily lives. Our lives extend past the day-to-day, here-and-now worries and chores. It is important to learn about Earth forces so we can fully understand how our actions influence or damage our environment. By using environmentally friendly cleaning products and recycling, we are working more harmoniously with our environment, and have taken the first step towards 'tuning in' to the universe around us.

The implications of our connection to the Earth and the universe have an important bearing upon personal healing.

Understanding how everything in nature and the universe relates directly to all human life on Earth gives us a new perception of who we are. Being in touch with our subtle energies links us to the universe and helps us develop a new sense of belonging, as we can feel that we are part of a greater whole.

Ego, Self and Soul – three perspectives

Before we go on to look at ways in which we can heal ourselves and become whole again, I would like to look at the differences between 'Ego', 'Self' and 'Soul', as it is important not to confuse these three concepts.

We commonly perceive ourselves as just a physical presence in this world, with a body that is governed by genetic information contained in our cells. This body is prone to illness if bacteria or viruses get a hold or when we are in a stressed state. When we are ill, we try to eliminate chemically – or, in the case of cancer, physically cut out – the invader or the diseased part.

As a physical presence in the world, we are also very dependent on our interactions with other people. If our relationships are good, we are happy, if they are unsatisfactory, we are distressed. We understand that other people's influence, both during childhood and in adult years, can make a great impression on how we feel about ourselves, and that at times it is necessary to analyse and work through past experiences that are still blocking us. We are also aware of our need for the approbation of others, and for the company of like-minded people.

It is within this traditional concept of existence that the terms 'Ego' and 'Self' are located. If emotional satisfaction can only be derived from our sense of being better connected, richer or cleverer than others, we are on what is commonly known as an 'ego trip'. This is not to be confused with the state of happiness that comes from *being* well connected, well off or clever. It is one thing to enjoy what you have; it is quite another to enjoy it only when you can show it off to others. The Ego is all about *being seen* to be something special or have something special.

Everyone starts with an Ego. Little children cry, 'Mummy, mummy, watch me!' to get attention and praise for some clever feat they are attempting. This is fine in children because they are learning new things and need to acquire self-esteem and confidence through the praise adults give them. In adults, however, a strong Ego is a sign of immaturity. (There is nothing wrong with having a moderate Ego as long as it is not all there is to you!)

In contrast to the Ego, a sense of Self is the inner picture we create of our person, which is governed by how well we relate to and connect with others – this Self-image is constantly modified by other people's reactions to us.

While the Ego will work from the premise 'I am the best and everyone else is inferior', the sense of Self checks and re-checks how I am actually doing in my relationships with others. With the Ego, there is no scope for realistic adjustment; with the Self, there is plenty, and if you are in the company of critical people, the danger of too much of negative adjustment may arise. This will lower your self-esteem and adversely affect your sense of Self.

One of the challenges in life is to find a good level of confidence and self-esteem which can hold up under unjustified reproof but can also take on board valid criticism so that we can modify our behaviour accordingly. In this state, we are in touch with our true Self. We feel rich emotionally. We are in touch with our feelings, we generally relate well to others and we like ourselves. We can set goals and, on the whole, are successful in achieving them. We are happy. This is the level where positive-thinking methods are so helpful in overcoming problems and obstacles that hinder our personal growth.

Both Ego and Self confine themselves, albeit in different ways, to a person's relation with their social environment and to the energies that come from other people. In contrast, the Soul is the part of a human being that relates to the bigger picture of life, connecting a person to the universe.

The Soul is that part of us that remains when our physical bodies cease to exist. It is our life force – the signature vibration of our unique person and personality, and as such, the Soul is the spiritual side of us. Nevertheless, it remains an intrinsic part of the physical body. The body cannot function in a coherent way without the energetic vibrations of the Soul, nor can the mind. Human beings are more than just the sum of their biological parts.

The Soul is part of but also separate from the physical existence of our body: it is pure energy, the vibrations of which interact with the physical body every moment of the day. It is the essence of our being. Homeopathy and flower remedies concern themselves with the essence of a flower or herb that is separate from the physical existence of the actual plant. The flower essence is the pure energy pattern of that flower. In the same way, our Soul is the unique vibrational energy pattern of our person which interacts constantly with all the other energy patterns in our environment and, on a larger scale, the universe around us.

The Soul provides us with vibrational energy, also known as life force, from the universe, but is also connects us to a higher plane of consciousness. Imagine taking a lift up into the sky and looking down on to the Earth: your perspective would change completely. The little everyday matters would no longer be visible and all that is left is the big picture. The Earth and all life on Earth is being put into the context of a much vaster realm – the universe.

Whereas the Self keeps our feet on the ground and helps us relate to others, the Soul lifts us out of the everyday and gives us a broader perspective. Being in touch with your Self gives you a high from living. Being in touch with your Soul gives you a high from being. On a spiritual level, your everyday sense of Self dissolves, the boundaries between you and others vanish and space and time lose their relevance. Just for a moment, rather than seeing the film of your life, you catch a glimpse of the light from the projector, leaving you with a sense of infinite space and inner harmony.

Keeping body and Soul together

In order to be happy within yourself, to feel centred and strong, no matter what your circumstances, you need to bring body and Soul together.

The body houses the mind and the emotions. It links us to the here and now and connects us to the people around us. The mind and the emotions link us into our everyday world, and this is a very important place to be! No amount of spiritual awareness alone will get you the right job, or the right partner, or help you out of a sense of alienation.

Work has to be done on a practical level to overcome trauma and sort out your emotions, and there is no way round that – you will find a great number of exercises in Part II to help you. Once your self-esteem and confidence are up and running again, you can become proactive and make the necessary changes in your life that will allow you to feel more connected to the world around you *and* happier inside.

Whilst you are working on your emotions, you can further help yourself rise above feelings of loss and distress by expanding your awareness beyond the everyday. By getting in touch with your spiritual side, you can begin to put problems into perspective and deal with them in a positive and constructive way. Nurturing the Soul creates peace of mind so you can get on better with your everyday tasks, and it can also help you progress faster when healing old wounds, be they psychological or physical.

As you work your way through this book, you will address both body and Soul, and you will find that it makes you feel calmer and more accepting of yourself, even though you are aware of shortcomings that you will still have to overcome. Bringing body and Soul together, we can achieve happiness, a feeling of belonging and the sense of being whole, no matter what our circumstances. Both body and Soul are essential if we want to experience our lives as fulfilling, if we want health and hope and a sense of being part not just of our immediate environment but also of a greater whole.

CHAPTER TWO

Why do we feel incomplete?

As we have seen, we define our Self within the context of our social environment. It is the presence and interaction with others that makes our Self three-dimensional. No matter whether these people relate to us in a positive or in a negative way, they will help us construct a picture in our minds of who we are. This inner image of our Self can only unfold if we can contrast ourselves against others. We need other human beings as reference points. Others function like a mirror in which we see ourselves, in which we see our Self. What others reflect back to us may be distorted, flattering, negative or positive, but at the very least it confirms our existence.

CASE STUDY

When Fiona came to see me, she was desperate. After her divorce five years ago, she had suffered a nervous breakdown and had been forced to give up work as a nursery nurse. Her energy levels were very low, she burst into tears at the drop of a hat, and everyday tasks such as shopping or cleaning her flat made her feel anxious and stressed. She had lost three stone within the first year after her divorce, but not because she was refusing to eat: 'I just don't feel hungry,' she said, 'I haven't had an appetite for ages.'

Fiona felt that after five years, she should be getting on with her life, but she seemed unable to climb out of the black hole of anxiety and depression she had fallen into. 'Even though my marriage was far from perfect, I have never experienced this sense of depression before. I feel like I have fallen apart, without being able to put the pieces back together again,' she explained. 'I am no longer the person I was before.'

Fiona's example may seem extreme but it is certainly not uncommon. What had happened to her was that she lost her sense of Self. Her thoughts and feelings revolved exclusively around the trauma of her divorce with the result that she was cut off from the world around her.

The constant assessment and reassessment of our person against the people around us helps us grow and develop. If we spend a lot of time on our own or withdraw for any reason from human company – if we are depressed or anxious, for example – we lose our outside reference points. On our own, we are at the mercy of our own thought processes, and these can begin to run unchecked so that fears and anxieties develop into a thing larger than life that threatens to overwhelm us.

Prolonged isolation from others can make us unhappy and, if there are pre-existing psychological problems, create mental illness. Once we have withdrawn into ourselves, we lose our Self – it is as if we have lost touch with the ground under our feet so that we drift through life out of control, at the mercy of our own unfettered thoughts.

Personality will of course also play a role. We may be a very intense person or the more easy-going type; we may be introverted, or we may flourish in the company of others. Depending on the people we meet and what happens to us in life, our personality can either make things easier or more difficult. Some people get stuck in their personal development and need help to unfold their true potential. Others find that time and personal insight allow them to become the best they can without outside help.

In this situation, it is important not to confuse losing your Self because you have lost touch with the world around you, and voluntarily seeking out space for yourself. Many people like to spend some time of the day in quiet meditation or choose to go on a retreat holiday once a year where they can withdraw from human interaction for a while in order to destress. This is very beneficial and a good way of grounding yourself and gathering new strength.

Our personality also determines how we *interpret* our experiences. However, this interpretation may have little to do with reality. If I am a very sensitive type and my boss gives me constructive criticism about a piece of work I have done, I may *construe* her comments as meaning that I have failed and consequently feel disheartened. Someone with a sturdier personality type may interpret the same comments as being a sign of interest and consider the boss's remarks as helpful. If there are many events in my life that I interpret as hurtful, I may end up wanting to detach myself from others.

Our past experiences as well as our personality decide how we interpret the way others react to us. What we regard as 'reality' and what, therefore, determines whether we are happy or not depends entirely on our subjective beliefs. We are of course influenced by our upbringing and by what we were taught by those who looked after us in childhood, but then *their* opinions and teachings were subjective too, as are the opinions and teachings of our present social environment.

As you go through early adult years, your acceptance of your parents' teachings is permeated by your own decisions about the meaning and value of things that surround you. As you get older, your personality and the culture you live in will determine how far you will shift away from what you have learnt in childhood and how far your personal belief system will differ from that of your parents.

Our perception of ourselves and of the world around us may appear static at any given point, and yet it can alter considerably over time. It is often only this shift in perspective rather than any change in circumstance that ultimately makes the difference between being happy and being unhappy.

The fact is that *we can choose* how we look at our circumstances and at life events. What happens in life can be painful, but whether we wish to suffer because of that pain is a choice we make. My stepdaughter Christina is a good example: she recently knocked herself very badly on a doorframe and burst out laughing, even though it clearly hurt her a lot. The last time *I* knocked my elbow on something sharp I got angry and felt really disgruntled about it.

Christina at fifteen had obviously decided that her little accident was funny, whereas I reacted as if something out there was out to get me. I was suffering, Christina was having a laugh. I clearly need to change my perception here because, to be honest, I'd rather have a laugh than suffer.

Think about your present-life situation. What is there that makes you unhappy? Have you been single for a long time? Are you unhappy with your looks? Are you stuck in a rut professionally? Are there people in your life that annoy or keep hurting you? Have you just lost your job? Or are you just unhappy without really knowing why?

If you feel that one or several aspects of your life make you unhappy, ask yourself whether your suffering is really necessary. The situation may be uncomfortable, hurtful or simply not what you want, but there is *always* something you can do about your circumstances. All you have to do is make a decision that you wish to change things and then go and do it.

Suffering is optional. There is no law that says that you have to suffer when certain things go wrong in your life, even when the experience is painful. Pain and suffering are two different things. When we lose our sense of Self, become disconnected and withdrawn, we lose sight of this fact – that we do have choice, that we can have control, and that we can change our life state. As we have seen from Fiona's experience, losing your Self is an involuntary occurrence in which you disconnect from the world around you because you feel you don't belong. It is usually a temporary state of existence, but it can become a problem if it continues over time. Let us now have a look at the reasons why this can happen.

Reasons why we feel disconnected

There are many circumstances and events in life that can cause us to feel cut off from our social environment and isolated within ourselves. Discontent, unhappiness and even illnesses can be triggered by psychological, physical and also by environmental problems.

On a day-to-day basis, you may already have become aware that your hectic life-style results in tension headaches or exacerbates another health problem you may have such as asthma or eczema. But did you know that some components of the beauty products you use regularly can disturb your hormonal balance? Or that all the electric and electronic equipment you surround yourself with can have a detrimental effect on your body's electro-magnetic field and make you feel disorientated, irritable and tired?

Psychological causes

Losing your Self and feeling isolated is not a trigger, it is a result. You may feel you are lonely because you don't have a partner, but loneliness is not reserved for singles. You can be surrounded by a large family or spend your working day in the company of a great many friendly colleagues and yet still feel lonely.

The cause of your loneliness may lie in your lack of confidence or your inability to communicate successfully with others. But why is that? How come you feel you cannot possibly go out by yourself or pick up the phone to ring a dating agency? The reason for this lies, in all likelihood, somewhere in your past.

You may have been conditioned to believe that only losers use dating agencies. Or a past event may have traumatised you so that your self-esteem has taken a knock and you feel awkward and reluctant when someone shows an interest in you. Other causes could be that your job is so stressful that you don't have the energy in the evenings or weekends to have a social life, or you may have manoeuvered yourself into a rut over the years and don't know how to escape old bad habits like spending all your evenings in front of the TV instead of going out.

Both past and present events can have an influence on how you relate to the world around you and how happy and contented you ultimately are within yourself.

Trauma

The influence of negative or traumatic past events on your personal development can have a disturbing effect on your sense of Self. Psychotherapy and conventional psychoanalysis is based on the premise that what happened to you in the past will have an effect on how you perceive yourself and your environment later in life.

Past causes can vary in their severity. We all appreciate that physical or sexual abuse in childhood can cause great psychological damage to a person. But less obviously traumatic events can also have a negative influence on our confidence and self-worth. Failing an exam is one example. You may go on to be a success in your chosen career, and yet the experience of that past failure can hold you back. Although you are achieving a lot in the present, you still don't feel that you are as good as everyone else. Some past events can leave their mark on you for the rest of your life unless you actively deal with their resolution.

As we have seen, personality will also come into the equation. Two siblings can give very different accounts of childhood years in straightened financial circumstances. One child may have experienced this time as very fraught and troubled, whereas another child remembers mainly the excitement of all the make-do arrangements. For some, traumatic events can be a disaster, for others, they bring positive solutions. When a past event has had detrimental effects on us, we may need to learn or relearn how to relate to ourselves and others in a positive way.

Typical signs that you are still struggling with something in the past are:

- Thinking daily about a certain past event.

- Experiencing flashbacks of a past traumatic event.

- Experiencing the same emotions today that you felt then.

- Having physical reactions as a result of thinking about the past event.

- Feeling your past has a hold over your present life.

Flashbacks and dwelling on past trauma can continue years after the original event has taken place. Persistent memories of trauma need to be released via conventional therapy or subtle energy work. If such memories are not released they will keep you locked in your past.

Conditioning

The way we relate to people invariably follows certain recurring patterns. These patterns are mostly established in childhood. When a trigger situation occurs, such as at mealtimes when a little boy persistently refuses to eat, the parents tend to go for their preferred way of acting in this situation (which often does not change greatly over the years). If the parents' habitual reaction is to shout at him or force him to eat, he either learns to comply and eat for fear of the shouting, or becomes even more stubborn. But he does not just modify his behaviour, he also learns about life.

The message the boy is getting is that if he refuses to do what someone in authority wants him to do, he is letting himself in for an unpleasant emotional experience – fear, resentment or upset. Depending on his personality, he will now begin to develop a particular attitude. This may say 'People in authority are bad news – avoid them/defer to them/obey them even though I may not want to', or 'I'm a bad person for not wanting to do what my mother/someone in authority wants me to do.' Any of these attitudes can then develop into a pattern for later life – conditioning has occurred.

Conditioning is not confined to family life. Our wider environment also has an impact on how we learn to see ourselves and the world around us. We are surrounded by publicity for products and life-styles, and these filter through into our perceptions. Body image is a good example.

A plethora of magazines and hoardings show us slim young models and well-honed male torsos. Is it surprising that losing weight seems to have become one of the major priorities for women and girls as young as six? Bulimia and anorexia are on the increase, and even boys are now occasionally affected.

Whilst there is no proof that advertising is *causing* these eating disorders, it certainly helps shape our perceptions and attitudes. As we are bombarded by images which we cannot avoid, a conditioning process is set into motion which, on a subconscious level if not on a conscious one, influences our views and therefore ultimately our actions.

CASE STUDY

Frank (aged thirty) came from a working-class family, with a depressed father given to rages and a mother who was cowed and anxious, and unable to defend herself against her husband's temper tantrums.

Frank had been suffering from mild depression for a number of years which became worse when he lost his job as a mechanic. He felt a failure and a freak, going from counsellor to counsellor to try to alleviate his feelings of depression and anxiety but without success. He was unable to sustain relationships with women because he felt disorientated in his role as a man. His self-esteem was also affected by the fact that the women around him, except his mother, were earning their own money and looking after themselves, so what was *he* good for as a man?

As Frank came from a dysfunctional family, his personal background was clearly a reason why he became depressed later on in life. In addition to the fraught domestic situation, his redundancy had contributed further to his sense of anxioty and insecurity. But another aggravating factor was that he felt he had no place in society.

As a man, Frank had been taught to expect to play the role of provider and protector. Although he managed to fulfil part of that role by defending his mother against his father, he was unable to be a provider, either for himself since he lost his job, or for a potential family. The fact that women did not seem to need him to look after them only made matters worse. Over the years, he had taken on board the messages his father gave him: a man needs to provide and a man needs to rule.

Detrimental relationships

Every relationship has its ups and downs. Over a period of time, you go through different phases with your partner, members of your family or friends. You may fall out with someone over a particular issue, someone may get on your nerves with their behaviour or mannerisms, or you feel they have let you down over something that was important to you. Differences of opinion can rock the boat, even over a prolonged period of time, but that does not make your relationship with the other person a detrimental one.

Relationships become harmful when being with the other person causes you physical or emotional injury. An obvious example is if your partner or another family member you live with is a substance abuser (alcohol, drugs) and becomes aggressive when in the grip of his or her addiction. But harm can also be done in much more subtle ways that are not necessarily obvious at first.

CASE STUDY

Nicole (aged twenty-five) had been going out with George (aged thirty-two) for a year when he proposed to her. 'It was all very romantic,' she said. 'He took me to a lovely restaurant, wined and dined me, and at the end of the meal, he got down on his knee, in front of all the other guests, and asked me to marry him. I was so happy!'

They were engaged for a year and then got married. Everything was fine. They got on well together. George was generous, affectionate and attentive. He rang Nicole at work every day, just to see how she was.

Nicole came to see me with anxiety and panic attacks. It turned out that she had become very insecure because George was checking on her every move. He rang her several times a day at work and wanted her to come straight home afterwards. When she occasionally wanted to go for a drink with colleagues or friends, he accused her of neglecting him, so she stopped going out. 'He even tries to stop me from seeing my family, and if I insist, he tells me that I put them before him and that I don't love him.'

George didn't hit Nicole, he didn't shout at her, and yet he damaged her emotionally. To an outside observer, he looked like the ideal husband who was charming, attentive and very much in love with his wife. In reality, his behaviour was destructive. He isolated Nicole from the social world around her, and as a consequence, she became nervous and anxious.

Nicole was confused because her husband seemed to love her and she loved him, and yet she had been unhappy since she married him. She wanted to see her friends and family, but she was worried about hurting George's feelings if she insisted. Maybe she didn't love George enough?

The following are signs of a detrimental relationship:

- Being sexually assaulted by your partner, even if it happens only once.

- Being physically assaulted.

- Living in fear that you might get physically assaulted.

- Being verbally abused.

- Being with someone who blows hot and cold.

- Being with someone who is a substance abuser and unwilling to seek help.

- Being with someone who is mentally ill and unwilling to seek help.

- Being ignored a lot of the time.

- Being frequently put down, ridiculed or criticised.

- Not being allowed to make your own decisions in matters that concern you.

- Knowing that you should leave the relationship but being unable to do so.

- Feeling normal when you are with other people and feeling crazy or complicated when you are with the person in question.

In any of the above cases, it is crucial that you get out of the relationship. It is fair to give the other person a chance to improve, but you need to realise that you won't be able to change them unless they can see for themselves that they have a problem. You won't be able to save them – only they can do that – so if they won't admit that they are in trouble, you need to leave or you will both go under.

Stress

Stress has been on the increase over the last twenty years. With the rapid developments in information technology, our lives have changed irrevocably. The pace of work has become more hectic and at the same time, people expect a higher standard of living than ever before. We work hard and we work long hours. If we have children, we want to be good parents and give them time and attention. This often leaves little or no time to think beyond the present work, family and financial issues.

Life is also more competitive. Parents now have to put their children's names down early to secure entry to a good school. Also, selection processes at high-profile universities have become more rigorous. When seeking employment later on, good positions are often fiercely fought over by a vast number of applicants, and with many more women having entered the job market over the last thirty years, competition has been hotting up even more.

We now have to study considerably more than in the past to keep up with the most recent developments in new technologies. If you want a good job and an above-average salary, it is no longer possible to stick with your initial studies throughout your working career. You are expected to keep abreast and update your knowledge if you want to progress.

Outside the family and work place, we need to cope with even more stresses. The daily commute to work forces us to share the pavements, roads and railways with a great many other people who are often harassed and impatient as they try and cram into an already overcrowded train compartment full of stale air. Aggressive behaviour in the streets, disruption on the railways, and congested roads and motorways make matters worse. We are bombarded all day long by a mass of information, only to come home and be fed even more information on the television. And then there is a problem with one of the kids.

We need to be more flexible today than ever before, but the constant changes can get us down and stress us to a degree where we hardly ever enjoy ourselves. Life is driven by the demands of work and family and all you can do is try to stay on top of it and just get through the day.

Feelings of anxiety are made worse by the fact that we are now more disconnected from our families and our fellow human beings. We live in smaller family units, with one-parent families commonplace, and we often live quite a distance away from members of our extended family. Our contact with neighbours is often spurious – you may chat several times a day to a stranger in South Africa via the Internet, but it is quite possible you have not spoken a word with your next door neighbour for the last six months.

Here are some signs that tell you that you are stressed:

- Lack of concentration.

- Forgetfulness.

- Lack of coordination.

- Indecisiveness.

- Making mistakes more frequently.

- Struggling with simple tasks.

- Mood swings.

- Excessive worrying.

- Shutting yourself off from others.

- Increased smoking/drinking.

- Overeating/not eating.

- Neglecting personal appearance.

- Obsessive thoughts.

Stress can alter the way we are, change our personality and temporarily obliterate our Self. We are merely functioning rather than relating to others; in fact when we are severely stressed we often shun contact with others because we cannot handle it.

Luckily, these extreme stress levels are mostly only temporary, and normality returns after a while. If extreme stress lasts over months, it can result in personality changes and will eventually take its toll, either on our mental or our physical health. It is therefore important to look at ways in which we can cope with unsettling events in a constructive and meaningful way.

The key to eliminating dissatisfaction and negative feelings is to pay closer attention to your inner world, and we will look at simple techniques in Part 2 to help you feel more positive and more alive.

Unexpressed creativity

Most of our everyday activities require predominantly rational thinking. We need to stay level-headed to make sensible decisions in order to get our work done efficiently at home or in the office. We need to organise our day wisely to fit in all the things that we want to accomplish. This lifestyle leaves little room for creativity.

You may be lucky and be in a profession that allows you to use your artistic talents, but even then your creativity is usually fettered by someone else's requirements, either your customer's or your employer's.

We are using the left, rational hemisphere of our brains to a far larger extent than the right, creative hemisphere. Although being reasonable and pragmatic is essential to make life run smoothly, it can tip the balance of your life too far towards head-driven activities. In order to feel whole and happy, we need both work *and* play.

Creative play is any activity in which you attempt the expression of your inner world in an unpressurised, enjoyable way. When you are playing games with others or learning a new skill, you are also being creative. The good news is that whatever creative activity you choose, it need not be anything useful!

When was the last time you did any of the following?

- Draw or paint.

- Sing.

- Dance.

- Write a story.

- Play an instrument.

- Play cards or board games.

- Learn a craft.

You can also express your creativity by being a little more adventurous in everyday life. Go into a shop and try on some clothes that are totally different from your usual style. Or take a completely different route home, just for the fun of it!

As children, we are creative all the time, but once we grow up, we often neglect this side of our existence. The most common stumbling-block people encounter when they try to put creativity back into their life is that they feel they need to be perfect when they attempt something. They put themselves under pressure to be 'good' at singing or dancing, or even just playing cards, and if they are not, they feel embarrassed and give up.

The beauty of creativity, however, is that its main objective lies in the expression of your inner world, of your imagination. Even if you need to practise scales on the piano, the sound of each key will evoke emotions and feelings that are often not addressed in everyday life. Playing a board game can be just as enjoyable and invigorating in a different way, as it gives you the opportunity to express in a light-hearted fashion sides of your personality that cannot be displayed in everyday life.

Creativity is a crucial aspect of a balanced life-style. You will find that a number of the exercises in Part 2 have a strongly creative component to them.

Life changes

You may have experienced something like this yourself. You were cruising through life quite comfortably when something happened that threw your whole being out of balance. You may have met someone and felt this person was right for you, either as a friend or as a partner, only to find that they were not what they seemed. Someone you were close to may have unexpectedly died, or maybe you lost your job and were suddenly faced with debts which you did not know how to repay. Life can throw the spanner in the works when you least expect it. When everything is running smoothly, it seems unimaginable that things could ever change, but they can and they do.

We live in a fast-moving and ever-changing world: there is no such thing as job security. Today, we often have had at least three different jobs by the time we get to retirement age. Fierce competition amongst giant companies makes life hard for smaller firms who must make great efforts to survive. Mergers and take-overs are now much more frequent, and these are accompanied by job losses.

Just as the job scene has changed, so have the basic building blocks of social structure. The divorce rate has increased. Twenty years ago, every third marriage ended in divorce; now it is nearly every other marriage. This means that today, many more people find themselves looking for a new relationship at a time when they had been hoping to be enjoying their middle age in the company of a loving partner.

The following are amongst the most stressful life changes:

- Death or grave illness in the family.

- Divorce or separation.

- Getting married.

- Redundancy.

- Retirement.

- New baby.

- Going bankrupt.

- Starting a new job.

- Taking out a big loan.

- Children leaving home.

- Moving house.

- Changing schools.

Physical problems

When our physical health is compromised, it has an automatic knock-on effect on our mind. Feeling unwell, being in pain or just coasting through the day on low energy levels makes you feel listless, exasperated and unhappy. We usually know when we are suffering from an actual illness, but few of us are aware of how much we are affected by the foods we eat and the chemicals that we use on a daily basis, such as those contained in beauty or household products.

Illness

An illness, injury or disability can be traumatic on a psychological as well as a physical level. For one thing, there is the issue of pain, and in particular chronic pain. Pain is extremely debilitating, as it takes up all your attention. You can easily become 'tuned in' to your pain to the exclusion of other things around you.

Your attitude is now crucial. With a positive attitude, you can heighten your pain threshold considerably, which means that you are less distressed by a certain level of pain than a person who has a negative attitude. With pain, your first priority will of course be to find and heal its cause, but if that takes a while, working on a positive attitude will be of great help.

Illness, injury or disability can mean we look or feel different from people around us, which can make us embarrassed, apologetic or gauche when in company. We can end up feeling a failure, and guilty for being ill. One consequence of this is that we feel we have to make up for our physical shortcomings. Alternatively, some sufferers take the attitude that they are owed something because of their physical condition.

In either case, our illness rules our interaction with people around us. Either we withdraw from others because we fear that people will look at our illness rather than at us as a person, or we want the company of others only to try and make them understand how much we suffer. Whichever is the case, we are not truly connected to others around us, nor are we in touch with our Self.

Allergies and intolerances

A rather less well-known source of disruption to your sense of Self is that of unrecognised allergies and intolerances. We are today bombarded by chemicals and irritants in our environment, both in the food we eat and in the air we breathe. Our bodies are forced to operate on high alert, with physical immune defence mechanisms working overtime for long periods during our waking and even sleeping hours. This means that the body has little time for rest and repair but is instead constantly on overdrive, fending off toxins from our environments while having to maintain everyday functions. This, together with a stressful life-style, makes us much more inclined to develop food allergies and intolerances, which in turn result in tiredness and irritability.

Today the most common food intolerances are to wheat and dairy products. When you crave a particular food, this is usually a sure sign that you have a high level of intolerance to this very food. This condition is also known as a 'masked allergy'.

Signs of a masked allergy are:

- The food in question is part of your staple diet.

- You crave the food.

- You feel very good while you're eating it.

- You feel a strong urge to have some several times a day.

- You feel irritable and out of sorts if you can't have any.

- You feel bloated after you've eaten it.

- You become irritable and restless soon after you've eaten it.

The allergy to the food creates a dependency which can only be broken by avoiding that food altogether for at least two months. This is no mean feat if you have a wheat intolerance, as lots of processed foods contain wheat. You will be amazed once you start reading labels!

Chemical overload

In April 2001, the *New Scientist* magazine reported that chemicals that mimic the effect of oestrogen are common in sunscreens, lipsticks and other cosmetics. Swiss researchers found that substances such as benzophenone-3, homosalate, 4-methyl-benzylidene camphor (4-MBC), octyl-methoxycinnamate and octyl-dimethyl-PABA can have a dramatic effect on animals. They trigger developmental abnormalities in rats and turn fish into hermaphrodites. UVB screening chemicals made cancer cells grow more rapidly as well as speeding up uterine growth well before puberty.

At the same time, hormonally active chemicals from the urine of women taking the contraceptive pill are already swamping the environment and may be causing a decline in sperm counts. Bubble baths, shampoos and shower gels often contain sodium lauryl sulphate (SLS) and sodium laureth sulphate (SLES). These are also used as engine degreasers and industrial cleaners, and are suspected carcinogens. Studies have shown SLS to have a degenerative effect on the cell membrane because of its protein-denaturing properties. Don't be deceived – many products labelled 'natural' contain SLS!

With artificial substances in so many everyday products, we can become overloaded with chemicals. We may believe we are only applying a substance to our skin, but in many instances, the chemicals contained in beauty products filter down all the way into the body. 4-MBC was even found in breast milk of lactating women.

Chemicals we use in the house or in the office can be similarly noxious. Cleaning materials containing bleach and other such substances are not only damaging for the environment, they also have a detrimental effect on our health.

As we are breathing in the fumes or vapours from photocopiers, printers, drycleaning fluids, paints and fire-retardant chemicals on upholstered furniture, we are exposing our bodies to a potential health hazard. And unless we experience an allergic reaction directly after being exposed to the chemical, we don't even know what is wrong when we start feeling unwell.

Chemical overload can create illnesses that are then treated with medication – which overloads the body even more, putting down layer upon layer of chemicals that stop the body, and ultimately the mind, from working properly.

Medication and recreational drugs

The average GP has little time to spend with his or her patients. In many cases, the consultation lasts as little as five minutes. GPs today have enormous workloads that do not allow them to go into great depth about patients' health problems. Medication is usually the fastest way to alleviate symptoms, either physical or psychological. But medication means feeding more chemicals into the body, and by alleviating symptoms, you are not necessarily sorting out the cause of a complaint. A study published in the *Journal of the American Medical Association* in 1998 revealed that adverse reactions to prescription drugs kill between 76,000 and 137,000 Americans every year, making it one of the commonest killers in the US.

No one can predict how your body will react to chemicals, be they prescribed medication or recreational drugs. Patients are often not made aware of potential side effects of medication they are about to take, and recreational drug users can never be sure that what they are taking is actually what the dealer says it is. Even though deaths from the use of recreational drugs are well publicised, users live in denial about the potential health consequences of their habit. For some, the wish to make life more exciting, escape from the everyday world or overcome shyness are overwhelmingly persuasive reasons to take the easy option.

Research carried out into the effect of cannabis (generally considered a harmless drug) revealed that it can lead to early psychiatric problems such as schizophrenia and paranoia. Having treated patients with drug-related physical and mental illnesses, I can certainly confirm these findings. Recreational drugs can lead to mind-altering experiences which change the brain chemistry in such a way that it leads to fears, phobias and stunted personal growth.

Let's look at a very common example of how alcohol is used to overcome a lack of confidence.

CASE STUDY

Gemma (aged fifteen) was in a clique of friends who went out together regularly at weekends. Everyone was drinking and everyone was smoking. Gemma, despite her verbal eloquence at home, felt quite timid when she was with her friends. She was very critical of her looks and her person generally and frequently referred to herself as 'thick'. When she was in the company of her peers, she admitted that she needed a drink or two to help her relax. 'Once I have had a couple of drinks, I don't care what I say or what I sound like. I suddenly find it much easier to talk and I'm having a much better time. Without those drinks, I feel really uncomfortable.'

As she used drink as a confidence booster, Gemma did not learn to increase her confidence through learning social skills that would help her communicate more easily with others. Her underlying lack of self-esteem was wallpapered over by the alcohol so that she ended up with low self-esteem and an unhappy liver!

Environmental hazards

We are today very aware of pollution, and much is being done thanks to the tireless work of pressure groups such as Greenpeace and Friends of the Earth. The Kyoto Agreement is a giant step is the right direction, but we cannot afford to relax as yet. There is a lot that still needs to be done to ensure that further damage to our environment is prevented and to repair what can still be repaired.

Besides pollution, I would like to introduce two other environmental hazards in the following sections that can also have an effect on our health and general well-being – electromagnetic disturbance and geopathic stress. These have only recently become better known to the general public, and many still consider them the imaginings of cranks, but there is now solid evidence that electro-magnetic disturbances and geopathic stress can affect your health. It is only a matter of time before they are acknowledged as forces that must be reckoned with.

Remember the days when those who spoke of global warming were considered alarmist and scientifically unsound? That was before the storms and floods ...

Pollution

When the word 'pollution' is mentioned, most of us think of the air we breathe, but this is only one of the problem areas. Oxides of nitrogen, sulphur dioxide, dioxins, carbon monoxide and ozone are emitted by automobiles, power stations, industrial plants and waste incineration sites, poisoning the atmosphere, damaging nature and destroying the ozone layer. As air pollution can be carried by wind, we all are affected by it, even though we may not live next door to a busy road or a big heavy industrial factory.

Also affected by the careless disposal of waste is the earth itself, which is contaminated by acid rain that brings down airborne pollutants. In addition, agricultural fertilisers and pesticides that seep down into deeper layers of soil are brought back up through the roots of plants that we end up eating later. Pesticides also get into our water, together with faeces and other solid waste that is still today often swept away through sewers into open waters without being broken down or cleared first.

There is also the problem of noise. At the moment, there are one million people in London alone who live under the Heathrow flightpath, having to endure a constant barrage of roaring aircraft engines overhead, with a plane taking off or landing every minute of the day.

On an everyday basis, you may have to put up with your neighbours playing their music too loudly at all hours, or sitting next to someone on a train who has turned up their personal stereo to full volume. And of course there are also the forever beeping, trilling, shrieking sounds of mobile phones or car alarms, and the incessant telephone conversations as you are sitting on a bus or train. All these are everyday stressors which are forced upon us and which grate on our nerves, adding to all the other stresses we are experiencing.

Electro-magnetic disturbance

Another source of physical disturbance comes from the great number of electric and electronic equipment we surround ourselves with, such as TVs, hi-fis, microwave ovens, computers, mobile phones and so on. All these gadgets emit electro-magnetic energies that interfere with the human body's own electro-magnetic field, with the result that we get unwell, can't think very clearly or feel permanently on edge.

A recent study in the US found that even a few minutes' exposure to everyday appliances can lead to depression, headaches, mood swings, anxiety, lack of concentration or low energy, as well as doing damage to your immune system and leaving you prone to disease. The American study revealed that brain performance and your health can be impaired by as little as five minutes' exposure to common domestic appliances such as TVs and mobile phones.

The following items could be detrimental to your health:

- TV equipment.
- Clock radio.
- Electric shaver.
- Electric kettle.
- Vacuum cleaner.
- Washing machine.
- Cordless phone.
- Computer.
- Treadmill machine at the gym.
- Sunbed.
- Microwave.
- Baby alarm.
- Electric blanket.
- Underwired bra.

There are simple self-help measures you can take to counter-balance electro-magnetic fields around you. Simply position yourself further away from the TV set, for example, or make sure you do not stand next to the microwave while it is operating. This will already help to reduce the electro-magnetic disturbance in your body.

Geopathic stress

The same happens when there is geopathic stress where you live or work. Geopathic stress is generated by energy disturbances that are located in the ground on which a building stands.

The Earth has a natural magnetic field which is produced by the molten metals in the Earth's core. The rotation of the Earth leads to the creation of electric currents in these metals, and it is this core electricity that produces a magnetic field. Human beings are used to living in this magnetic field and resonating in harmony with it, so disturbances in the Earth's electro-magnetic field can have a detrimental effect on our health.

Disturbances can occur through geological faults, underground ore masses and underground water, as well as mining shafts, foundations of tall buildings that go deep into the earth and any other tunnelling systems such as sewage, water pipes and underground transport systems.

In addition, there is a global grid network of electrically charged lines criss-crossing the Earth's surface, called Curry and Hartmann Lines. In places where these lines cross, the Earth's electro-magnetic field is often disturbed and can have detrimental effects on people whose houses or offices are built above the crossing lines.

There are many more causes of geopathic stress, but all of them have one thing in common – they have an ill effect on energy levels, emotions and health. Amongst the effects of geopathic stress are:

- Disturbed sleep.

- Waking up feeling tired and irritable.

- Restlessness.

- Inability to get well after an illness.

- Immune system problems.

- Miscarriages.

- Infertility problems.

- Birth defects in babies.

- M.E.

- Headaches.

- Hyperactivity.

- Some cancers.

CASE STUDY

Karen (aged forty-two) had noticed that since she had moved to their new house, nearly every member of her family had started getting ill. Her young daughter started developing serious stomach problems, she herself was feeling depressed and very tired through lack of sleep and her son, a formerly good student, was starting to have problems concentrating. Just like her children, Karen spent a lot of time in the house, whereas her husband was out all day at work. After living in the house for a while, Karen also heard that three of her neighbours were seriously ill with cancer and another person had recently died of the disease.

Karen had heard about geopathic stress and decided to investigate. She had a dowser come to her house to find whether it was indeed geopathic stress that was responsible for her family's ill health.

The dowser found that the entire neighbourhood, including Karen's own house, was riddled with geopathic stress. Karen discussed the matter with her husband and they decided to move. Once they were in their new house, the family's symptoms began to clear.

Karen's story is an extreme one. Very often, a lot can be done by moving a bed to a different position or by using crystals or metals to rebalance the Earth energies under a house. There is more about possible solutions in Part 2 of the book.

What happens when we are disconnected

Any life event will affect us where we are most vulnerable. If your physical health is a little fragile, a detrimental life event will most likely manifest in deteriorating health. If we are psychologically vulnerable, we will be more susceptible to fears, phobias or depression. But the effects of fragmentation can be much more subtle still, and this can make them harder to combat. Even when we have everything we want – a good job, a loving relationship, all the holidays and possessions we could desire, as well as a great circle of friends – we can still feel that something is missing.

Depression and anxiety

Depression and anxiety often go hand in hand, making you want to withdraw from the world. As you lose touch with others, you live only in your thoughts, endlessly going over past events, endlessly worrying about what you have to do next, getting agitated about things that happened in the past, replaying old memories, thinking about what you should have done or said. Anger against yourself and others is often a big part of depression. And as you are withdrawing from the world outside, your feelings can run unchecked and gain enormous and unrealistic proportions. You tune out the world around you, you lose your Self and become your depression.

Signs of depression are:

- Hopelessness.
- Difficulty concentrating.
- Indecisiveness.

- Not laughing any more.

- Feeling angry inside but suppressing it on the outside.

- Losing interest in aspects of life that used to be important to you.

- Feeling agitated.

- Fidgeting and feeling compelled to move around.

- Feeling constantly tired.

- Having to make a big effort to do even simple things.

- Feeling anxious in the presence of others, even friends.

- Feeling anxious without knowing why.

- Feeling like a failure.

- Disturbed sleep or sleeplessness despite tiredness.

- Feeling trapped.

- Feeling depressed even when good things happen.

- Changes in your normal eating pattern (overeating/not eating at all).

- Feeling suicidal.

Any feelings of grave sadness which last for more than two weeks need professional attention. If you find that you have some or all of the above symptoms, and especially if you feel suicidal, then see a therapist and use this book as additional self-help in support of your therapy.

It is possible to overcome depression, and there are many good and efficient therapies which will be able to help you get better (see Resources, page 183).

Resentment, anger and violence

When you are overloaded with emotional stress, be it through past trauma, low self-worth or because you feel that others have taken advantage of you, inner pressure starts building up and eventually you will either implode or explode. When you implode, the inner pressure creates depression (see page 56) or it manifests as illness.

If you have a tendency to keep your emotions in, you can end up with feelings of resentment. Someone has hurt you, ignored you, treated you with disdain or made you feel small and you cannot forget. The event could have happened yesterday or twenty years ago – the feeling of helplessness and frustration inside is the same.

CASE STUDY

Nicole (aged thirty) was about to get married to her boyfriend John (aged twenty-eight). Her mother, who had moved into her own flat after living with Nicole for a year, kept ringing Nicole several times a day and came to visit several evenings a week.

Nicole had a full-time job and wanted to relax in the evenings. Instead, she got involved in long telephone conversations with her mother, who depended on her daughter for social contact. In addition, Nicole's mother was agoraphobic and unable to leave the house by herself, so Nicole needed to help her with the shopping, take her to the doctor's and generally run errands for her.

Nicole felt resentful and angry about her mother's constant demands and need for attention. Since the problems had started, she smoked so much that it made her sick at times, but she was unable to give it up. 'The cigarettes are my reward for putting up with my mother,' she said. 'They help me keep the lid on my anger.'

If you cannot or will not address your grievance with the person concerned, your resentment smoulders and gradually builds into anger. This is then often released towards a third party who has nothing to do with the original event. Some people take out their anger on other motorists while driving, others take it out on their colleagues at work or their partner and children at home.

We all get angry once in a while. That is quite normal and part of everyday life. When it happens on a regular basis, though, it is time to do something about it.

Warning signs are:

- Obsessive thinking about particular past events.

- Persistent angry feelings in the stomach area.

- Being unable to concentrate on anything besides your angry feelings.

- Feeling you are about to explode.

- Wanting to let off steam by hitting someone or damaging something.

- Shouting a lot.

- Using alcohol, cigarettes or drugs to keep your angry feelings at bay.

In extreme cases, people are unable to control their anger and become violent. When body and mind are overloaded, release comes in the shape of physical action. Once the aggression has run its course, there is a sense of relief, often followed by regret and shame. In other cases, where someone has no sense of self-respect or respect for others, the violent action will result in a sense of power and self-importance which then leads to further episodes of violence. To end this, it is essential to look at and work through what has happened in the past so that the inner pressures can subside and a sense of self-worth start to develop.

Loneliness

When you look around you at people you know, your friends, acquaintances and work colleagues, you will probably find that quite a number of them are single or divorced and live on their own, some with and some without children. The papers and magazines are full of lonely hearts advertisements, dating agencies and tips about how to find a new partner. Even though there is less of a stigma today about being single, the unhappiness of being without a partner remains a problem for many.

When you are longing for a special relationship but you feel that this is not within your reach, it is as if part of you is missing. When I did research for my book on singles in the 1990s, I found that most people interviewed wanted a new relationship, and their happiness as a single appeared to depend on how optimistic they felt about achieving this aim.

Those who were desperate to find a new partner reported experiencing a much greater feeling of loneliness than those who took a more relaxed attitude about their single status and could enjoy the advantages of being on their own. Another aspect of this is the fact that desperation clearly makes for unwise choices, so that unhappy singles often ended up with unsatisfactory new partners.

Loneliness is not the same thing as being alone. You can have lots of friends, a loving partner and children and still feel lonely. Equally, an inattentive partner can be just as demeaning to your sense of Self as can being single. Think back to when you were a teenager: you were surrounded by your family, and yet you felt lonely and misunderstood.

CASE STUDY

Amanda (aged twenty-one) had been married for three years to Wayne (also aged twenty-one) and they had a little girl of three, Charlene. Their relationship was strained at times because Wayne liked to disappear to the pub after work to spend time with his mates rather than come home.

Amanda resented his absences because she felt very unsupported and lonely, sitting at home with their little daughter. 'The way Wayne is treating us, I might as well be a single mother,' Amanda said. 'I have a husband, but he is never home. I can't go out because of Charlene, and most of my friends have children as well and cannot just come over in the evenings. I feel very isolated and lonely.'

Loneliness is also a matter of perception. Depending on how good you feel you are at relating to your fellow human beings and, above all, how well you feel they relate to you, you will experience a greater or lesser extent of loneliness. When you do not feel connected to others because of a lack of positive feedback, your Self is not nurtured, and your own doubts and fears can get the better of you.

The way forward needs to be positive action, no matter what the reasons are for your sense of loneliness. If your lack of confidence or self-esteem stops you from saying what you want to say or from connecting with others, you can either work through the exercises in Part 2 or you can seek professional help.

Even if, as in Amanda's case, your partner is the one who 'creates' your loneliness, you can still benefit from being more focused and centred within yourself. The more self-assured you feel, the more effectively you can communicate your needs to your partner. There is always a solution, even if you can't see it at the moment.

Rootlessness

If you want a career today, you often have to be very flexible regarding the number of hours you work and where you work. A general downturn in the economy, as well as a great number of mergers and takeovers in industry over the last ten years, have resulted in mass reorganisations and redundancies. The modern marketplace demands an employee who is willing to uproot his or her entire family to fit in with working requirements. Gone are the days when you stayed in one job and in one place throughout your working life!

Moving house means uprooting yourself from your home and having to settle in all over again in a new environment. We may not have great community spirit any more these days, but we still have friendly neighbours, a helpful postman, work colleagues and friends somewhere in the vicinity, and we lose all this when we move with the job. It can take years to rebuild all these social contacts in the new environment. Do you know anyone who still lives in the same town where they grew up?

Also, families today are smaller than they used to be thirty years ago. In some areas of the UK, nearly 50 per cent of school children come from one-parent families. Relatives do not necessarily live nearby any more, so that grandparents cannot give a hand with childcare if both parents are working. And of course it also works the other way around – children are no longer nearby to look after their ageing parents.

For most people, the family support network can no longer be relied upon. But even if the whole family stays together, a repeated change of location can be very unsettling, especially for children who lose their schoolfriends every time they move.

There are also increasing numbers of people who choose to work freelance. In the course of their work, they may be dealing with many different customers or companies, but at the same time, they are never really part of any particular firm.

Even when you are given a temporary office on your customer's premises, this is not the same thing as belonging. People know you are only there for a limited period of time, which is often not long enough to establish good social contacts or make friends. You are surrounded by people, but you don't belong. If, at the end of the day, you are returning home to your family or partner, this will help, but if you get back to an empty flat because you are single, it can be a lonely experience.

In order to overcome feelings of rootlessness, it is essential to feel at home within yourself. In some professions, there is not a lot you can do about a vagrant lifestyle if you want a career, but there is a lot you can do that will help you to feel connected with the world around you, as you will see in Part 2.

Emptiness

This is an inner state that can develop at any stage in life and is independent of social status. We can have health, wealth and good relationships, and yet still fall prey to this feeling. When everyday tasks and events lack meaning or when we feel our life has lost its purpose, we may experience this sense of discontent. When we lose a sense of meaning, we lose motivation and enthusiasm for life.

Signs of emptiness are:

- Feeling unfulfilled by work.

- Loss of purpose.

- Listlessness.

- Shunning human company.

- Inability to laugh.

- Feeling that something is missing in your life.

- Feeling you are just going through the motions at work and with family and friends.

Attributing meaning to what we do is something we learn when we are very young. Parents praise their children's actions, and this helps them give meaning to their activities later on in life. It is, for example, important for babies to get a reaction from parents when they throw toys out of the pram. When a parent verbally comments on the baby's action and returns the toy to the pram, the baby begins to develop the realisation that they can have an effect on their social environment and so develop a sense of Self.

Dependency

This comes in many guises and is not always easy to recognise. It can develop from psychological or physical causes, or sometimes from a combination of both. Alcohol abuse, for example, can happen as a consequence of psychological factors such as peer pressure, stress, past trauma or a lack of confidence, but it also involves the physical aspect of craving, and just like food allergies, the craving is often an indication that you have an allergy to that particular type of alcohol that you cannot get away from.

Any of the signs below indicate a problem with alcohol:

- Being unable to go without a drink even for a single day.

- Being drunk regularly.

- Needing a drink first thing in the morning.

- Being secretive about the amount you drink.

- Becoming irritable or aggressive if you can't have a drink.

- Needing a drink to relax.

- Using drink as comfort on a regular basis.

Clearly, with this sort of dependency, the psychological causes need to be addressed as the drink takes the place of comforter, companion and ego-booster, and often also functions as a release from stress.

Just as alcohol dependency has been around for decades, so has drug abuse. One time, it was laudanum and the opium pipe, now it is Ecstasy, amphetamines and cocaine. The worrying trend is that recreational drugs are on the increase and have now become socially acceptable in many circles.

In April 2001, the *Independent* newspaper published the results of research that showed that 50 per cent of UK youngsters between the ages of fourteen and nineteen had tried illegal drugs. The cigarette behind the bike shed is still number one, but other addictive substances such as cannabis, uppers, 'Charlie' and other drugs are fast becoming regulars with teenagers.

The signs for drug dependency are similar to those for alcohol abuse:

- Feeling you can only be yourself when you have used the drug.

- Feeling that your enjoyment of a social event is diminished unless you take drugs.

- Finding you can only keep going if you take drugs.

- Finding you can only relax if you take drugs.

- Craving the drug.

- Being unable to attend any social event without taking drugs.

While large quantities of alcohol are certainly detrimental to the drinker's health in the long run, recreational drugs can be severely damaging, and perhaps lethal, even if you do it only once. At my practice, I have seen cases of paranoia, bulimia and other severe psychological problems that were induced by short-term or even one-off use of a recreational drug. Extensive therapy was necessary in all cases to restore normal mental health.

These, of course, are extreme examples, and it is not within the scope of this book to deal with drug-induced cases of psychosis or any other psychosis, nor can the exercises described here be a substitute for professional psychiatric or psychological treatment if you suffer from clinical depression or feel suicidal. However, even if you suffer from any of these more severe conditions and are receiving conventional treatment, this book can be a valuable addendum to any therapy you are undergoing. Extreme mental states *can* be sorted out, but they will need some solid professional help in addition to the exercises you will be reading about next.

In Part 2 of the book, we will be looking at how we can attend to *all* aspects of our being in order to create inner happiness. You will learn how to access both body and Soul to help you heal, recover and gain inner happiness by using positive thinking, visualisation techniques, healing movements and energy techniques.

PART TWO

Becoming Complete

Introduction to Part Two

In Part 1, we have explored what it is that makes you feel complete, and the reasons why this inner equilibrium can be disturbed so that you end up feeling distressed and unhappy. Let's now move on to the solutions!

Part 2 is divided up into two chapters. The first chapter helps you deal with past events that have resulted in you developing a negative self-image, a detrimental thought pattern or an unproductive perception of the world around you. By doing the exercises in this chapter, you are 'tidying up' your past. There is no point in building a new house on a ruin – before you can create something new which you want to be solid and permanent, the old 'rubble' needs to be shifted out of the way! This will leave space to construct a new, positive awareness of your Self.

The second chapter helps you to access and heal every individual aspect of your Self – body, mind, emotions and Soul – step by step, so that you can create the inner harmony necessary to achieve happiness. You can now begin to build your new life on a good and solid foundation, focusing on all four life aspects in turn to bring them together and make a harmonious whole.

Please remember: it is not enough to just think a few positive thoughts or concentrate on the body only. True and lasting happiness will always require a balanced interplay between body, mind, emotions and the Soul.

Both the first and the second chapter require you to follow a variety of different exercises. Some will ask you to use visualisation, which involves drawing on your mental resources, others will consist of energy techniques that teach you how to change your physical and mental vibrations into positive ones. Every exercise is marked clearly to tell you exactly what level you are working on.

Clearing up the past

In this chapter, you will be working on those issues in your life that linger on from the past and have been building up into stumbling-blocks that are holding you back today.

In order to overcome them and begin the healing process, we need to look at a number of potential problems. First of all, it is necessary to find out if there is a negative *life pattern* that we are following. This will give us clues as to where we need to make changes in our lives. In this chapter, we will explore what life patterns do, why they can be useful and what action to take when they become detrimental.

We can then go on to look at ways in which past experiences manifest themselves in our present-day feelings and actions, and what effects these have on our perception of our Self. Here you will find a test to help you establish whether your past is still ruling your life today, as well as exercises to help you move forward in your life without baggage.

Depending on your past experiences and the patterns that govern your life, your *thoughts and mental images* may or may not be helping you achieve happiness and health. As thoughts and images usually work on an automatic, subconscious level, they are often hard to detect and therefore difficult to change for the better. I have devised a test as well as exercises to help establish the areas in which you can improve, and go about changing negative into positive.

In the final part of this introduction to healing, I have set out exercises to help you rebalance body and mind through a *change of perception*. By shifting your point of view and becoming proactive rather than being sad and depressed about what is wrong in your life, you can re-establish meaning and put your life and your Self back together again.

The exercises in this section work at both a mental and a physical level. When the exercise asks you to visualise something, you will be working at a mental level. As we have seen, mental visualisation has a knock-on effect on the body, emotions and energetic vibrations. This means that any visualisation covers all the four essential life aspects – body, mind, emotions and Soul. The same is true of the physical exercises that follow. Even though, on a conscious level, you are only working on the body, you will at the same time improve your mental state, calm your emotions and enhance the energy vibrations of your Self.

Eliminating negative life patterns

Life can become very difficult when events outside our control disturb our emotional equilibrium. Traumatic events can lead us to harbour negative emotions about ourselves, with negative thoughts and images going around in our minds, often continuously. When this goes on over a long period of time, it can make us ill.

Losing your Self does not happen out of the blue, but as a knock-on effect of stressful conditions and emotional trauma. As a consequence, a negative life pattern is set up that can detrimentally affect every aspect of your life unless you are able to deal with the stress or trauma in a constructive way.

CASE STUDY
Zoe (aged thirty-eight) had had three major relationships in her life. None of them had been happy. She had never

married because, according to her own assessment, she had a great fear of being abandoned and an equally great fear of leaving a relationship herself. Her first partner had been constantly unfaithful, and although this had hurt Zoe a great deal and they had had many rows over his behaviour, she had felt unable to break off with him until *he* finally left *her*.

Zoe felt suicidal, but was 'rescued' by another man who helped her through the break-up and then became her new partner. But this relationship also turned sour, with her new partner trying to control everything she did. Again, rows ensued and the man finally left.

Zoe had a nervous breakdown, which she overcame with medication and counselling sessions, only to land in yet another relationship that made her unhappy. Her partner criticised her a lot and made her lose even more of her already damaged self-confidence. They rowed, he packed his bags, but every time he was about to leave, Zoe caved in and begged him to stay because she was terrified at the thought of being abandoned.

Zoe's fears went back to having been ill and left in hospital for two weeks when she was eighteen months old. She had been crying incessantly, and even a kindly nurse who picked her up frequently and carried her around had not been able to comfort her.

On a logical level, the adult Zoe could understand where her fears originated, but on an emotional level, this knowledge did not help her change her negative life pattern. In her sessions, it turned out that Zoe had been treated in a very disrespectful way by her father when she was younger. He had constantly criticised her and put her down. Even though her mother was witness to these put-downs, she had never taken Zoe's side so that Zoe ended up believing that she was a worthless person. She had picked her partners accordingly! It took Zoe quite a lot of hard work in her sessions with me, but she finally came

> through and left her unsuitable partner. She has now found someone who respects her and treats her well.

Patterns as such are not a bad thing. We need certain routines in life to be able to cope with the multitude of tasks most of us have to deal with on an everyday basis. Your weekday pattern may be to get up at a certain time in the morning, take a shower, get dressed, have breakfast and then take a particular train to be at work on time. These routines may be boring or tiring, but they are necessary to impose a sense of order on our daily activities. Time management patterns are desirable, simply because they keep the stress levels down.

Then there are behavioural patterns, which are very much tied in with emotions and arise out of our past experiences. These behavioural patterns can work to our advantage or to our disadvantage. If I always ask for an explanation when I don't understand something, I will be getting answers to my questions. If I don't dare ask when I don't understand something, I end up getting things wrong and making mistakes. My behavioural pattern of asking when I don't understand is therefore very useful, because it clarifies a situation so that I can stay calm and relaxed.

Some behavioural patterns are only temporary because they are linked up to a certain phase in our lives. Teenagers, for example, often go through a phase of moodiness, rejection of parental authority and general anti-social behaviour, but once they have found their feet as adults, they usually revert back to being human! It is the knowledge (or hope) of the temporary nature of their children's objectionable behaviour that tends to keep parents sane.

What we need to explore in this section, however, is the bigger picture. We all have emotional patterning that dictates our behaviour in certain situations. The question is: is there an *emotional routine* that runs like a red thread through your life and makes you react unreasonably to certain situations? You know that you are locked into a negative life pattern when you seem to make the same mistakes again and again or when the same unpleasant things keep happening to you. Typical negative life patterns include, for example, starting things and never finishing them, constant worrying, staying in untenable situations even though they are clearly bad for you or, in terms of health, suffering from recurring illness or health problems.

To establish if, or where, you are trapped in a negative life pattern, do the following test. Go through each statement carefully and grade it according to how true it is for you. If a statement reflects 100 per cent your own thoughts, give it a grade 5; if the statement is completely untypical of your way of thinking, give it grade 0. The grades are as follows:

Grade 5: That's exactly how I feel!
Grade 4: I frequently feel like this and it makes me very anxious.
Grade 3: I sometimes feel like this and it bothers me.
Grade 2: I sometimes feel like this but it doesn't bother me.
Grade 1: I rarely feel like this.
Grade 0: This thought would never cross my mind.

Write your grade down next to each statement. You will need it later on to evaluate your progress.

Checklist

1. When someone else is in a bad mood, it affects my own mood in a negative way. ☐

2. I don't feel that I have control over my life. ☐

3. I doubt very much that I will ever excel at anything. ☐

4. When something goes wrong during the day, it depresses me for a long time after. ☐

5. My life is ruled by my sense of duty towards family, friends and employer. ☐

6. I'm expecting my future to be as unsatisfactory as my past. ☐

7. I have developed thought patterns that make me unhappy. ☐

8. I have behavioural patterns that I dislike but cannot stop. ☐

9. My daily life is at the mercy of my feelings. My feelings are unpredictable. ☐

10. I seem to do all the right things but never get the results I want. ☐

11. I have habits that make me feel a failure. ☐

12. I am unable to say 'no', even when others make demands that are clearly unreasonable. ☐

13. When certain situations occur in my life, they trigger great fear in me, even though other people don't seem to be bothered by the same situation. ☐

14. It is important to me to do everyday things *always* the same way. ☐

15. I hate conflict and will avoid it at all cost. ☐

16. I'm fearful of most things in life. ☐

17. I feel that others are better than me. ☐

18. I suffer from a particular health problem that keeps recurring. ☐

19. There are things I could do to improve my life situation, but I'm not doing them. ☐

Use the grades as points and add them all up.

0–15: You are doing very well. You are generally in good emotional balance, so your life pattern looks fine.

16–30: There are some minor problems in your life pattern that need addressing. Doing the exercises in this book will be very helpful, so get cracking!

31–60: Your life pattern begins to mar your enjoyment of life.

Make sure you do something about it *now* before it starts getting out of hand. Work on the exercises in this book *regularly* to get back in control of your life.

61–100: Alarm bells are ringing, but you know that yourself already. Use the exercises in this book consistently and, if you cannot get to grips with your negative life pattern on your own, get professional help. Useful addresses are given in the back of the book on pages 183–9.

Each of the above statements is a sign of a negative life pattern, so the more of them you said 'yes' to, the more firmly you are caught up in detrimental routines. If you have marked statement 18 as applicable to you, you need to check whether poor health goes hand in hand with emotional problems and also whether your environment disturbs your electro-magnetic field (see page 53).

Clearly, the higher your overall grade, the more problems you are having with negative life patterns. If your score is high, don't let this discourage you; on the contrary – once you have established that your life pattern is part of the reason that you are unhappy, it gives you a much clearer picture of your status quo. Also, understanding which issues are a problem to you can lead on to a tailor-made solution. As long as you are vague about what is bothering you, you cannot make a determined effort to overcome it. You need a clear aim to arrive at your destination, and you also need to know exactly where you stand right now.

The reason why I want you to write down the grade for each individual statement is that you will need these grades to check your progress once you have worked through the exercises in the following chapters.

A negative life pattern can occur in any area of your life. It affects your relationships, work, health, your ability to perform and your potential to thrive as a person. A detrimental emotional routine is a sign of fear, and fear makes you inflexible. In order to allow your energies to flow freely again, you need to let go of fear and anxiety and influence your emotions favourably by doing the following exercise.

The psoas exercise

This is a mental exercise that uses visualisation to help the body relax.

Before I introduce you to the actual exercise, I would like to explain some anatomical detail about this very powerful method of self-healing, for to do the psoas exercise well, it is important to understand what is going on in your body. The aim of the exercise is to release a particular muscle called psoas (pronounced 'so-es'), which is at the core of your body. The main function of this important muscle is to flex the hips and keep the lumbar curve in the spine.

The psoas muscle is associated with the kidney meridian. In fact, the kidneys rest on and to the side of the psoas muscle. This meridian is associated with fears and stress reactions.

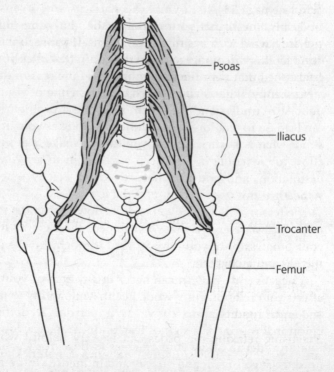

Psoas

Iliacus

Trocanter

Femur

The position of the psoas muscle.

The psoas links the lumbar spine to the top of the legs, and when the psoas is functioning well, it has a beneficial effect on the circulatory system, the functioning of the organs and diaphragmatic breathing. It also massages the vertebrae and inner organs while you are walking.

When you feel afraid or stressed a lot of the time, the psoas contracts and your body goes out of balance, both physically and in energy terms. This disturbance shows itself as restricted motion and joint movement, including your diaphragm. Equally, if the pelvis is unstable or off balance, the psoas muscle must contract to make up for the lack of support to the spine, ribcage, neck and head. Only by contracting continuously can all these structures above the lower back be kept stable.

When the psoas is chronically used in this way, it loses its flexibility and shortens. Once this happens, the organs in the body become squashed together as the taut psoas pulls the pelvis forward, thus restricting the space available in the pelvic region. This will impinge upon nerves, impair diaphragmatic breathing and cause digestive problems.

Conditions that make your psoas constrict are:

- Shoes that fit too tightly.

- Shoes that won't let the foot roll when walking.

- Shoes that limit ankle mobility.

- Seating that does not support the lower back.

- Premature standing and walking and not enough crawling in babies.

- Fear and anxiety.

- Stress and trauma.

- Mental rigidity.

Practising relaxing the psoas can be very helpful when you are 'stuck' in a life situation, pattern or habit. Getting in touch with the psoas muscle, your inner core, will not only be physically beneficial by making you feel more grounded and centred, but it will also have a positive effect on your emotions. Releasing the tension in your psoas has a stabilising effect on your mood.

But now on to the actual exercise.

What to do

- Lie down on your back, legs pulled up and hip-width apart. Rest your hands on your abdomen or next to your body. If you find it more comfortable, you can let your knees rest against one another.

- Gently massage the two points which are situated one inch above and beside the navel (see illustration below) for about ten seconds. These are the neurolymphatic points relating to the psoas muscle. By massaging these points gently, you help the lymph relating to the kidney meridian move around the body.

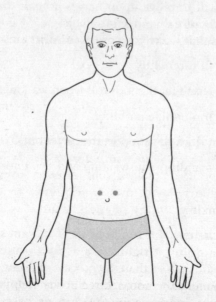

The positions of the two neurolymphatic points relating to the psoas muscle.

- Close your eyes and lie still. Concentrate on your spine in your lower back and imagine the psoas muscle fastened to each side of the the lower spine and extending to the top of your legs. Picture the psoas lengthening and smoothing out and sinking down on to the floor or bed beneath you.

How long does it take?
Ten minutes twice daily, on waking up and before going to sleep. Also a good exercise if you cannot sleep.

What's the aim?
To get in touch with this core region of your body. To relax and release the tension in the psoas so it can become flexible again.

How do I know I'm doing it right?
You will either find you are taking spontaneous deep breaths in when your psoas is beginning to relax, or you feel tension drifting out of your lower back.

What to avoid
Pressing your back down purposely. Allow the psoas to let go of tension in its own time.

Troubleshooting
I cannot imagine the psoas. Imagine instead that you could hear the inside of your back creaking as if a rusty mechanism was beginning to grind into gear after someone had applied oil to it. Or imagine someone had put a pleasantly heavy weight inside your abdomen, making your lower back very heavy and causing it to sink down towards the floor. In this version, concentrate on imagining a physical feeling.

I have done the exercise for a few days and am still not sure whether I am doing it right. This doesn't matter. Pay attention to the results rather than the process of doing the exercise. If you feel calmer and more relaxed at the end, you are doing something right, so keep doing it, whatever it is!

As we have seen in Zoe's case history (see page 70), it is past experiences that shape the way we live our lives. But past experiences do not only shape our life patterns; they also result in us developing a certain Self-image that can slow us down in our personal development or even prevent us from being happy. In the following section, we will be looking at how we can overcome trauma from the past in order to establish a positive perception of our Self.

Overcoming a limiting past

Both our life patterns and the thoughts that fill our minds make us distinct from other people. As a human being, each one of us is truly unique. There may be people around you who are like-minded, who have the same values and even a similar personality, who speak or dress or look like you, but no one is exactly like you.

Developing and maintaining a sense of Self is dependent on the presence of other people to whom you can relate, either in a negative or in a positive way. How you relate to the people around you will depend on two factors: your personality and your past experiences. Our personality is established with conception when the blueprint from our mother's and our father's genes merges into a new human being which is physically and mentally similar but not the same as the parents. We are born with likes and dislikes, with a particular temperament, with behaviours that are typical for us and that express our personality. From the day of birth, children who are born to the same parents can be totally different from one another. This means that personality is a factor in your Self perception which is original to your person and as such independent of your social environment.

On the other hand, there are our past experiences. Everything that happens to us from the day of our conception to the last day of our lives is processed by our mind, and this processing creates emotions. Any new information that comes from the outside world will be compared to previous experiences and then categorised under a particular heading. Let's take the example of a little girl who grows up in a loving environment. She experiences positive attention, warmth and affection a lot of the time. This helps her develop a belief that, basically, the world is a safe place where she can have an influence on what is happening. Now she starts school with a very harsh teacher who finds fault easily and criticises frequently.

This is new information that does not fit in with the old experiences, and the view that the world is a safe place full of warm friendly people now has to be adapted to accommodate it. Depending on her personality, she may now start getting anxious or calmly make efforts to work harder, or she will refuse to go to school. At the same time, she will also start thinking and feeling differently about herself when she gets criticised for making a mistake. She may now start feeling insecure, unsure of her ability to cope with the work in class. She may lose confidence or she may rebel. The new experience has not only resulted in her reviewing her view of the world, but it has also affected her behaviour and her view of herself.

New experiences are seen through the filter of personality and are compared to previous experiences. If a new experience does not fit into an existing category, it is often stuck into a category that is the closest match. If I'm two years old and my mother shouts at a me, I interpret this as meaning that she doesn't love me any more, so this event goes in the emotional category 'rejection', notwithstanding whether I have just done something that frightened my mother or whether my mother is suffering from PMT today. There is no 'PMT' category in a child's mind, so the shouting goes into the 'rejection' box. One of the challenges of growing up is to learn about different categories, and children often have to learn this by themselves, without explanations from adults.

Experiences form inner beliefs, and these beliefs will determine how you behave and what results you are getting. Beliefs act as a guiding life structure which allows you to make sense of what is happening to you. Beliefs are at the basis of any life pattern that you eventually establish. Often, just one short experience can be enough to change your view of the world totally, with the result that you alter your behaviour to the opposite of what it has been before.

Milton H. Erickson, an American psychiatrist, liked to illustrate this point by recounting the story of a male orderly who worked on a maternity ward and who loved drinking milk. He had had a glass of milk every day for the twenty years that he had worked at the hospital. One day, a nurse pointed out to him that the milk he had just consumed had been mother's milk that someone had left in the fridge. The orderly never touched milk again.

It is the same with other events in your life: one sentence, one experience that only lasts a few minutes, can influence your belief system so drastically that it entirely changes the way you view yourself. Consequent alterations in behaviour can then lead to changed outcomes in the area of mental and physical health, personal and professional performance, the quality of your relationships with others and the way you perceive yourself. Outcomes can then have a feedback effect on your personality – an unhappy experience can make people who used to be outgoing become shy.

Within the context of this book, I would like to define 'experience' as anything that makes a significant impression on your emotions, be it in a pleasant or unpleasant way. There are four main categories of negative experience which can lead to a loss of Self.

- Failure
  - failing an exam/test
  - failing to live up to someone else's expectations
  - failing sexually (impotence/frigidity)
  - not getting promoted
  - failing to find work
  - failing to do the right thing

- Loss
  - loss of work
  - loss of partner through divorce or illness
  - loss of someone close to you
  - abortion and miscarriage

- Rejection
  - by a prospective employer
  - by parents
  - by a partner or a potential partner
  - by friends or colleagues at work

- Trauma
  - verbal abuse
  - physical abuse
  - sexual abuse
  - being deserted
  - being kidnapped, mugged or assaulted
  - witnessing violence against someone else
  - witnessing or being involved in frequent rows and arguments
  - accident
  - severe illness (mental or physical)
  - operation
  - being in physical pain over a prolonged period of time

As negative experiences can have a major impact on your well-being, check with the next test whether any of the following statements apply to you. Just as you did for the previous test, I would like you to read through each of the following statements and grade them according to how relevant they are to your situation.

Grade 5: This statement applies to me 100 per cent.
Grade 4: This statement reflects how I feel quite often.
Grade 3: I sometimes feel like this and it upsets me.
Grade 2: I sometimes feel like this but it doesn't bother me.
Grade 1: I rarely feel like this.
Grade 0: This statement does not apply to me.

Write down your grade next to each statement. You will need it later on to measure your progress.

Checklist

1. I feel compelled to think about certain past events in my life, even though this upsets me. ☐

2. I'm scared that I will go on having the same negative experiences that I had in the past. ☐

3. I have developed thought patterns that upset me. ☐

4. Although I hated the way I was treated by others in the past, I seem to be treating others in the same unacceptable way now. ☐

5. I have done something in the past that made me lose all self-respect. ☐

6. I have omitted to do something in the past that I should have done. This omission has blighted my life since. ☐

7. I often have unexpected flashbacks about a past traumatic event. ☐

8. I cannot remember anything before the age of ten. ☐

9. I have a chronic illness and now I feel guilty because someone said that I have attracted the illness through negative thoughts. ☐

Use your grades as points and add them up.

0–18: No problems for you, especially if you are at the lower end of the scale. It is still worth your while going through this section and learning how to do the exercises as they are excellent stress-release techniques. That way you will have them ready should you ever need them.

19–30: Your past is having a negative influence on your mind, body and spirit, especially if your score was at the higher end of the scale. You are not fulfilling your full potential, so make sure you work through the exercises thoroughly in this part of the book. If you do, you will see good results.

31–45: Your past is ruling your life. Work with the exercises to get back some control. If you feel you are not making sufficient progress within the next two weeks, get professional help.

Before we move on, I would like to look at each statement in turn.

1. I feel compelled to think about certain past events in my life, even though this upsets me. Rerunning old memories over and over again in your mind can become a kind of addiction. This is an emotional coping mechanism to help you get over a hurtful event, but it is as if the memory tape got stuck on a permanent repeat loop. This is frustrating, debilitating and tiring.

2. I'm scared that I will go on having the same negative experiences that I had in the past. The future can change any minute. There is no guarantee that tomorrow will be the same as today. Your past is clearly governing your expectations, and this can make you behave in a way that makes your expectations come true. Use the psoas exercise (see page 76) to change the pattern to positive. Releasing the physical tension around the psoas will help you release mental and emotional tension too, which frees up your way forward to the adoption of a more positive attitude.

3. I have developed thought patterns that upset me. It is important to become aware of what event has caused this thought pattern to evolve and to establish exactly what that thought is saying. This is something you can do right now – write down those upsetting thoughts in direct speech – for example, 'I'm just not good enough.' Then start thinking about when you started to believe this thought. Who taught you that you are not good enough? Becoming aware that this is not your own thought but someone else's is often helpful in getting a perspective on that thought.

4. Although I hated the way I was treated by others in the past, I seem to be treating others in the same unacceptable way now. You can see how the experience-outcome chain worked for you. What happened to you established a memory trace in your mind that turns into an automatic response whenever you are in similar situations. Something you used to loathe in the past still has a hold over you in the present. Learn to change your life pattern by doing the psoas exercise (see page 76). Later exercises in this section will also be helpful.

5. I have done something in the past that made me lose all self-respect. It is okay to review your actions, but it is not useful to dwell on them or feel guilty about them for years afterwards. You will be better off making efforts to ensure you won't make the same mistake again – this can then help rebuild your self-respect. Later exercises in this section will help you relax and overcome your feelings of guilt.

6. I have omitted to do something in the past which I should have done. This omission has blighted my life since. Use your past failing as a learning experience, not as eternal punishment. Make amends where you can instead. Imposing an inner life sentence on yourself does not help anyone.

7. I often have unexpected flashbacks about a past traumatic event. This is a sure sign that your mind has not come to terms with the trauma, and the flashbacks are a warning sign that you need to disengage from its emotional content. The exercises in this section will help you achieve this.

8. I cannot remember anything before the age of ten. This is not necessarily a sign of repressed trauma. Some people do not have a very good memory for past events, and many people remember little before the age of six. Do check though whether you really don't remember anything: try thinking about a house or flat you lived in before the age of ten, a school build-ing, a child in your class. Sometimes more recollections come back once you have grabbed one memory. On the other hand, if the attempt to remember brings up disturbed feelings, there may be repressed trauma which you might want to tackle with professional help.

9. I have a chronic illness and now I feel guilty because someone said that I attracted the illness through negative

thoughts. It is not true that you create your own illness. What can happen is that things occur in your life that you experience as traumatic. This stress then translates into a physical imbalance that can cause chronic illness. This is different from you causing the illness. If you cannot let go of the guilty feelings, use the meridian tap (see page 91) to help you.

If a past event still has a hold over you, the next two exercises can be a great help in lessening its emotional impact. Both exercises are based on kinesiology and the meridian system. They are an adaptation of Thought Field Therapy which was developed by Dr Roger Callaghan, an American clinical psychologist. He discovered that when you tap particular acupuncture points on the body, it helps people overcome, amongst other things, phobias and post-traumatic stress. The method works on a vibrational level, clearing disturbed energy frequencies in the body's meridian system so that previously upsetting thoughts can no longer create emotional distress.

When past events still feel like they happened yesterday, even though they go back a long time, the upsetting emotions have not been processed by your mind. The collarbone breathing exercise allows the body and mind to relax, whereas the meridian tap enables you to let go of the emotions that still accompany the memory of the past event. That does not mean that you will forget that the traumatic event happened. You still know what went on in the past, but you can now be emotionally detached from it.

CASE STUDY

Rachel (aged twenty-three) had found out two years ago that her boyfriend was two-timing her. She had felt that Ian was her ideal partner, and there had been talk of an engagement before she made the discovery that Ian had been seeing another woman for the last two months. Rachel was heartbroken, angry and hurt. She was unable to eat for weeks after the split. 'My mind is still occupied with going over and over my relationship and break-up with Ian, even now, two years after the event,' Rachel told me when she came to see me. 'I can't stop thinking about him; it's like an obsession. I'm no longer who I used to be.'

I explained the collarbone breathing and meridian tap exercises to Rachel and we went through these in the session. Even while we were doing the meridian tap, Rachel started feeling that her distress levels were coming down. At the end of the session, she confirmed that she felt much better. I gave her the exercise as homework, and a few days later Rachel rang me to say that she had started going out with her friends again and was having a good time.

Here are the two exercises I taught Rachel. Before starting, look at the illustration opposite to familiarise yourself with the points that you will need to tap, rub or touch later on.

Collarbone breathing exercise

This technique uses two kidney acupuncture points beneath the collarbone to help body, mind and emotions calm down.

This is a good exercise to bring general stress levels down. Use the collarbone points shown in the illustration opposite to do this exercise. These points are significant because the kidney meridian runs through them. By breathing consciously whilst holding these points, you help balance the subtle energies going through your body.

What to do

1. Rest three fingers of your *right* hand in the hollow underneath the *right* collarbone while you breathe as follows:

   – take a deep breath in
   – breathe half way out
   – breathe all the way out
   – breathe normally for one breath cycle

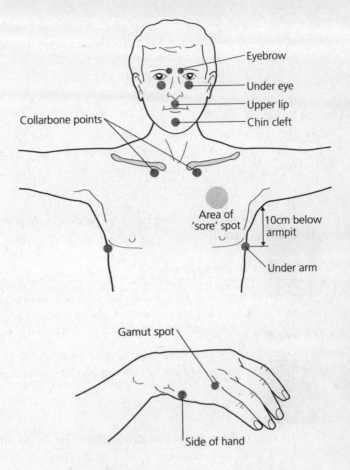

*The positions of the collarbone points and
other acupoints on the body.*

There is no need to hold your breath at any stage. You can do this sequence quite quickly. One cycle only takes a couple of seconds.

2. Rest three fingers of your *right* hand in the hollow underneath the *left* collarbone and breathe as before.

3. Rest three fingers of your *left* hand in the hollow underneath the *left* collarbone and breathe as before.

4. Place three fingers of your *left* hand in the hollow underneath the *right* collarbone and rest the fingers there. Breathe as before.

Repeat these steps another four times.

How long does it take?
Do this exercise whenever you feel stressed and also before doing the meridian tap. Once you know the sequence by heart, it should not take you more than three minutes to do it.

What's the aim?
This vibrational breathing exercise helps to calm and relax you mentally and emotionally.

How do I know I'm doing it right?
You will feel calmer and more focused when you have finished the exercise.

What to avoid
Getting too hung up about where exactly the points are. As you are using three fingers, one of them is bound to be in the right place.

Troubleshooting
I can't find the right points on the collarbone. Find the knobbly bit of your collarbone on each side. These tend to stick out a bit when you are slim. If you are well padded around your chest area, you need to dig a bit to find them. If you now put a finger on the knobbly bit and then slide the finger off downwards and slightly sideways, away from the midline, you will find a small indentation. This is where you should place your three fingers.

Do the collarbone breathing a couple of times to become familiar with it. It can be done quite quickly once you know where the fingers need to be placed. You can do the collarbone breathing on its own for general stress, or before you do the meridian tap.

Meridian tap exercise

This energy exercise helps to release fear from body and mind.

The meridian tap is very useful if there is something in your life you are afraid of, or if you are upset by a present or past situation. The meridian tap will help you reduce the fear you feel and allow you to let go of your distress. The tapping of the various points helps rebalance the body's meridians so that a previously upsetting thought becomes neutral. This helps the body to relax, the mind to stay focused and the emotions to remain calm around the memory of something traumatic.

First of all, look at the following scale:

10 Distraught and beside yourself; severely depressed; unable to function.

9 Distraught and only just about able to function in everyday life.

8 Very upset and crying a lot, feeling devastated.

7 Very upset, crying occasionally, no longer feeling yourself.

6 Upset and unhappy, but still yourself.

5 Unhappy.

4 Sad.

3 Able to think about an event and only feeling vaguely sad.

2 Okay.

1 Feeling over it.

0 No particular feelings any more when thinking about the trauma.

Now close your eyes and think about the traumatic or anxiety-inducing event. Right now, whereabouts on the scale is your upset when you think about it? Make a note of the rating.

Now we come to the actual tapping sequence. *It is essential that you think about the trauma while you tap the points.* Better still, speak the thought out loud while you tap. Rachel, for example, said 'Ian left me' while she tapped.

Use both hands and tap each point between five and ten times. You can do so rapidly. Think a short sentence referring to your problem or say it out loud while you tap.

1. Find the sore spot on the left side of your chest as indicated in the illustration on page 89. (Note: you may find that the sore spot is in a different place next time you do this exercise.) Repeat your short sentence three times while you are rubbing the sore spot. Now, whilst saying/thinking the sentence:

2. Tap the inside of your eyebrows.

3. Tap under your eyes.

4. Tap under your nose.

5. Tap under your lower lip.

6. Tap under your arms.

7. Tap your collarbones.

8. Tap the side of your hand (one hand is sufficient).

9. Tap the top of your hand (one hand is sufficient) and do the following:

   – close your eyes
   – open your eyes
   – hum a few bars of a tune out loud
   – count 1-2-3-4-5 out loud
   – hum a few bars of a tune out loud

10. Repeat steps 2 to 8.

Now close your eyes and think your upsetting thought again. Where on the rating scale are you now? The rating should have come down now. Repeat the tapping sequence 1 to 9, then 2 to 8 again, if necessary several times, until the rating comes down to an acceptable level or, ideally, 0.

How long does it take?
About two to three minutes for a full round of tapping, which means tapping 1 to 9, then 2 to 8. Do this several times a day or whenever you start getting upset about the past event.

What's the aim?
To disengage old emotions from the memory of a past event. To lessen anxiety levels.

How do I know I'm doing it right?
Your rating will gradually come down and you will notice that you are feeling less and less upset when thinking about the past event.

Troubleshooting
I've done the meridian tap religiously, but my rating is not really coming down. You may have to be more specific about the past event. Many traumatic experiences have several facets to them. In Rachel's case, she needed to tap for six different sentences: 'Ian cheating on me', 'Ian leaving me', 'Ian lying to me', 'Ian being happy now while I am unhappy', 'I'm angry' and 'I'm desperate'. Make sure you tap for every single facet of your particular problem. You will only achieve substantial improvement when all aspects have been tapped for!

Overcoming past trauma or unsettling events is a very important part of putting an end to negative patterning in life. Sometimes, however, we can still be left with the habit of negative thinking even when we have put the past behind us. This negative outlook can be like a scar after an accident – even though the accident happened a long time ago, the scar stays as a reminder. In the next section, we will be tackling any limiting thoughts you might have developed as a consequence of past experiences.

Transforming emotions through positive thoughtforms

In this section, we will be looking at the power of thought and how we can harness it to get well emotionally, physically and spiritually. We rarely question our thoughts or enquire where this or that thought comes from. Do thoughts originate in the brain or do we receive them from another source inside our bodies? Are we actually affected by the thoughts of others around us? We seem to be blindly accepting the thoughts and ideas that are ruling all our everyday actions. And yet, conscious and subconscious thought is frequently not only the cause for illness but also the cause of healing. Thoughts evoke feelings, and feelings trigger physical and mental responses. Thoughts can make us ill, but they can also play a crucial part in healing us.

Try the following experiment

- Ask a friend to stretch out one arm to the side at shoulder height and get her to say out loud, 'I am weak and pathetic!' three times.

- Gently press her arm downwards at wrist level and notice how easily her arm comes down.

- Now get your friend to shake out the arm and ask her to take a few deep breaths.

- Ask her to hold the same arm out as before and get her to say out loud, 'I am strong and confident!' three times.

- Again, apply the same gentle pressure downwards to her arm and notice how much stronger the arm is. You will find that the arm will now be much harder to push down than before.

What has happened here? Depending on what your friend said about themselves, the muscle tone responded accordingly. The negative statement made the arm weak, whereas the positive statement made it strong. This experiment is actually a very simple form of kinesiology which shows how the body reacts with weakness or strength depending on whether the thoughts or words are negative or positive. In this context, it makes no difference whether you believe what you say or not. Even when someone just *thinks* these sentences, their arm will react accordingly.

This simple experiment shows how important it is that we work at becoming positive and constructive. Your subconscious mind is always listening and will act on information you have spent a lot of time thinking about. This means that when you occupy your mind with negative thoughts about yourself or your situation, you are actually weakening your body, thereby making it both harder for you to succeed and more difficult for your body to function properly. The body–mind connection is always working, either to your advantage or to your disadvantage, depending on the thoughts that fill your mind.

When we speak of 'thinking', this can involve a number of quite diverse activities. We may mean that we are consciously exploring the solution of a problem by thinking it through rationally. 'Thinking' could also refer to dwelling idly on thoughts about someone we know, an old memory or recent events. We can also let our thoughts drift forward in time and imagine what our future will look like in five years. All these activities we describe as 'thinking', even though quite a few of them will involve not just verbal activity, but also images. In order to encompass both verbal and pictorial thoughts, I will use the term 'thoughtforms'.

Most of the time, we think automatically rather than purposely, and therefore we are rarely aware of *how* we think and in which way our thoughts present themselves in our minds. We are often more conscious of the feelings that our thoughts evoke than the actual wording of the thought or the image that accompanies it.

Upsetting feelings are frequently the first warning sign we get that what we are thinking about is disturbing our emotional equilibrium. You are thinking about a mistake you made recently and you feel embarrassed. You are thinking about a boring job you will have to do and you feel exasperated. You are thinking about a healthcheck you have booked for the coming week, and you feel afraid. This is not to say that these are the only possible reactions you can have to these situations, but if you react with fear, embarrassment, despair or other forms of distress to a particular thought, then you have a problem that needs to be tackled.

Thoughtforms affect us on all levels. Whatever goes through the mind will automatically filter down into the body and affect the subtle energy of the meridians, either in a positive or in a negative way, depending on whether the thoughtform is optimistic and happy or pessimistic and depressed.

CASE STUDY

David (aged twenty-six) was terrified of being away from home. Whenever he needed to travel, be it to go on a holiday or occasionally on business, he felt physically ill. He described it as a 'big cloud descending' on him that oppressed him for at least a week before the dreaded travel date. He had to consume a considerable amount of alcohol or take tranquillisers in order to cope with the journey away from home. His symptoms were less severe when he went to a place he had been to before – he still was nervous but not as frantic as he was when he had to travel to an unknown destination.

David had no recollection of a particular event that had started this negative pattern for him – he had suffered from this problem since he was a schoolboy. I therefore started working with him on the thought processes that were going through his mind before the start of a journey. We found a number of fearful thoughts that resulted in his feeling depressed and anxious before travelling. The thoughts he identified were 'there is no help out there' and 'I will leave everything familiar behind'.

I explained to David that these were protective thoughts that were set up by his inner self-preservation mechanism to ensure he was safe. For some reason, his mechanism had gone into overdrive at an early stage in his life, and it was this over-reaction that was causing him the problems.

The thought 'there is no help out there' should really say 'make sure you have help out there'; the thought 'I will leave everything familiar behind' was another way of expressing 'everything is unknown and strange out there' which, of course, is true when you have not been to a foreign place before. David's thoughts were accompanied by images of being stranded with a broken-down car, ill in a foreign hospital where he did not speak the language or unable to find his way around. He had developed this fear after having been shunted from home to home as a child.

David had to relearn how to think in a more constructive and helpful way about travelling. It took him quite a while to change his automatic panic into happy anticipation, but he succeeded in doing so with the exercise you will find later on in this chapter (see page 99).

Before you tackle this exercise, I would like you to check whether you have any negative thoughtforms that are blocking your progress in life. How many of the following statements could you attribute to yourself? Grade each of your responses to the following statements as follows:

Grade 5: This is exactly the way I think.
Grade 4: I often think like that.
Grade 3: I sometimes think like that and it bothers me.
Grade 2: I sometimes think like that but it doesn't bother me.
Grade 1: I rarely think like that.
Grade 0: This thought would never occur to me.

Write down your grades next to each of the statements. You will need them later to check your progress.

Checklist

1. I would rather be anyone else but myself. ☐

2. I have brief moments where I see disturbing pictures in my mind which do not seem to relate to anything I have experienced in my life so far. ☐

3. I have been trying to think positively over a long time, but somehow, it doesn't work for me. ☐

4. When I look back over my life and think of where I am today, I am dissatisfied. ☐

5. My thoughts are automatically negative most of the time. ☐

6. I cannot see a future. ☐

7. I don't think I can visualise. I just don't have any imagination. ☐

8. I don't like who I have become. ☐

9. I don't think others like me. ☐

10. I dislike myself and I resent others. ☐

11. Whatever anyone else says about me stays in my mind for years afterwards, but only if it was something negative. ☐

12. I feel it is important to hide my inadequacies from others around me. If they knew the real me, they would lose interest or reject me. ☐

Use the grades as points and add them all up.

0–24: Your thoughts are generally optimistic and you have a positive view of yourself and your abilities. Great – keep it that way!

25–40: It would be to your advantage to do some work on the quality of your thoughts, especially if you are at the higher end of the score. There is no need to put up with unhappiness produced by negative thoughts. Get going on the exercises as soon as possible.

41–60: Your thoughts are getting out of hand and are making your life a misery. Make sure you work steadily with all the exercises in the book to help yourself out of your negative frame of mind. If all else fails, let a good therapist help you.

The chances are that if you have discovered a negative life pattern by doing the test on page 73, you will have been able to relate to quite a few of the negative thoughts in this section. You will have noticed that most of the statements highlight how you *think* you relate to yourself and others. If you believe that you are inadequate in some way or if you compare yourself unfavourably to others, then this will distort your behaviour and therefore negatively influence the reactions you are getting. Please be clear about one thing: just because you *believe* something about yourself does not mean it is *true*!

Your beliefs are often established in younger years and can prove to be quite persistent, even in the face of facts that clearly contradict them. Look at a person who has a cat phobia. No matter how many of his friends demonstrate to him that their cat is friendly and gentle, he will not go near the animal.

So what can you do to influence your thoughtforms in a positive way? You will find the following exercise helpful in freeing up energy that at the moment is tied up in being afraid, over-critical and stressed.

Self-preservation reset exercise

This is a mental exercise using visualisation to help resolve inner conflict.

Negative thoughtforms may be a nuisance but they do serve a purpose. They are there to help you become a better person, to be cautious and sensible. In addition, they also serve to help you avoid getting hurt. The only drawback is that these thoughts may be simply too extreme and mar the quality of your life. It is like squashing a gnat with a sledgehammer if you don't speak up at a meeting because you might stumble over a word or because everyone will be looking at you. More crucially, it is an over-reaction to refuse to have a social life just because you feel you are not as good as everyone else. Your inner self-preservation system has gone haywire and needs resetting.

What to do

- Make yourself comfortable and close your eyes.

- Get in touch with the inner self-preservation thought that makes you unhappy or prevents you from doing what you want to do.

- Imagine taking the thought out of your head and making it into a person who addresses you with those negative words.

- Decide what this person's good intention is. What are they trying to protect you from?

- Thank the person in your mind and ask them to encourage you instead.

- Shake hands on the deal and then reintegrate your self-preservation part back into yourself.

Let me run you through an example by telling you how David (see page 96) dealt with this exercise. If you remember, one of his negative thoughts about travelling was 'there is no help out there'. When David took that thought out of his mind, he saw it as a gnarled old man who shook a finger at him.

David decided that the old man was probably trying to protect him from all the unpleasant eventualities that might occur on his travels, such as the car breaking down, getting ill abroad or losing his way. David thanked the old man for his good intention and negotiated a new thought: 'Make sure you have all your insurance in place and a good map!'

After having done the exercise a few times, David was able to detect more easily when the old negative thought was coming up and was able to replace it consciously with the new thought whenever the fear arose in him. It goes without saying that he invested in a good travel insurance and a map before setting off! Thought without action remains ineffective.

How long does it take?
About five to ten minutes. It is fine if you need longer though.

What's the aim?
To become aware of the protective function of negative thoughtforms and achieve a more moderate version of the thought.

How do I know I'm doing it right?
Before you do the exercise, think about the thought that is making you unhappy. Do this whilst resting a hand on your navel. Check how your belly area feels. You will notice an unpleasant sensation, such as tingling or butterflies.

After the exercise, think the new, more moderate thought with a hand on your navel and check again how your belly reacts. You should now experience a pleasant or neutral sensation under your hand. If the feeling is still unpleasant, you need to repeat the exercise because you have not yet found the right replacement thought.

What to avoid
Getting too hung up about seeing everything clearly in your mind. A vague sense of knowing what this inner thought looks like as a person is good enough.

Troubleshooting
I don't get a person, I get an animal/a cloud/a fairy tale figure. It doesn't matter. As long as the thing can speak, you are in business. Start negotiating a better deal!

I can't find a better alternative to the old negative thought. If a good friend came to you and complained about the same negative thought, how would you change that thought for him or her? Decide and then take your own advice!

The old negative thought keeps coming back! Of course it does! If you were a thought that had settled comfortably in someone's head, would you just go? Certainly not. Keep at it! Say the new thought several times a day, several times in a row so that it gets deeply imprinted into your subconscious mind. Be as stubborn as the old thought, and you will get results.

Improving your life by changing your perception

Two people can have the same experience, but when you hear their accounts or observe their reactions, you might see or hear very different responses.

Two men working for the same company who are being told that they have been made redundant can respond in completely opposite ways. One of them may become angry or distressed and lose his confidence so that he feels unable to look for a new job, whereas the other man may be just as shocked to start with but then rallies around, inspired by a new challenge.

Two women may both find out from their doctor that they have cancer. One of them may be traumatised and immobilised by her fears, the other one deals with the traumatic news by looking into all the possibilities that are open to her to combat the illness.

How we tackle something that is wrong in our lives will depend entirely on our point of view. There are always different angles from which we can look at a problem, but we are often too entrenched in our old ways of thinking to be able to make the necessary adjustments. And even if we want to look at things more positively, we may not know how to go about it. How do we change our perception?

CASE STUDY
Philippa (aged thirty-six) sees herself as a loser. She is single and works for social services where she is doing a

difficult job with a great deal of dedication and success. She has good friends and is popular with her work colleagues, and yet suffers from low self-esteem.

Her problems started when she was learning to play the violin as a child. Her parents, unable to afford to buy a new instrument, gave Philippa her grandfather's violin when the little girl said she wanted to learn to play.

Together with another four pupils, Philippa started lessons after school once a week, but she soon felt very unhappy. Her teacher gave his entire attention to another girl in the class while ignoring his other pupils. Philippa was struggling with learning to handle her violin and was getting no help from her teacher.

After half a year, she gave up because she felt she would never be able to master the instrument, and ever since then, she had felt a failure.

At first, when Philippa recounted her story during a workshop, this seemed a straightforward case. Discouraged by the teacher's lack of interest in her, she had given up when she was not making any progress. As I felt that it was important for Philippa to get a new perspective on the problem, I did the following exercise with her.

The screen exercise

This mental exercise uses visualisation to help you gain a clearer perspective.

What to do

- Single out the memory or current situation you are struggling with, either because it makes you sad or embarrassed, or because you cannot stop thinking about it for any other reasons.

- Close your eyes and think the memory/situation through from start to finish, remembering as much detail as you can.

- Now imagine you could take the memory/situation out of your head and put it on to an inner screen so that you can watch the memory/situation like a film.

- Watch the goings on in the screen as an outside observer, and notice how you can see things differently.

How long does it take?
As long as you need to get a new perspective.

What's the aim?
To become more detached from a formerly distressing memory. To get a more neutral perspective on an issue that you feel confused or uncertain about.

How do I know I'm doing it right?
When you feel better or clearer after having done the exercise.

Troubleshooting
I am still unable to get a different perspective, even though I put my problem situation on my inner screen. You may have to picture your memory in context. This can mean having to make the film longer by adding what happened beforehand. If your girlfriend put you down in front of your friends last Saturday and you reacted very angrily, you may not be sure whether you have been over-sensitive or not.

In this case it would be useful to check whether you have any earlier memories of your girlfriend doing the same thing. If she did, and you can link together several similar memories, your reaction is appropriate. If she never put you down in front of others before and if, in the one-off situation when she did, she apologised once she realised she had hurt your feelings, then your distress was understandable at the time but is no longer useful to you now. Should you still have problems letting go of the memory, do the meridian tap (see page 91) to get rid of your resentment.

With Philippa, I went through the screen exercise as follows. I asked her to close her eyes and imagine she could see the old memories of her violin lessons on an inner screen. She was to be merely an outside observer watching an old film. I then asked her to describe to me what she could see on the screen.

As Philippa began to watch her old memories as a film, she suddenly exclaimed, 'The violin is far too big for the girl!' Looking at the past event with objectivity, she could now see that there was no way that she could have learnt to play the violin because her hand was too small to span the neck of the instrument. No wonder she had had difficulties learning to play!

I asked Philippa to imagine going into the screen and telling the teacher off for not spotting this problem. Philippa also felt she wanted to have a go at the teacher for behaving unprofessionally and not giving all the children equal attention. Once she had done this, she felt a lot better. 'It is like a weight has been lifted from my mind,' she said afterwards. 'It wasn't my fault. The violin was just too big!'

The screen exercise is very useful if you want to get a more detached view of a present or past situation. Do you feel you over-reacted the other day when your boss asked you to work late? Do you feel your husband is not giving you enough support at home? Put it on your inner screen to see all the angles of a situation so you can find a more helpful perspective.

Swapping places

Sometimes it can also be useful to explore an event from another person's point of view in order to change your perspective about what has happened or is happening. By understanding where the other person is coming from, it becomes possible to appreciate their reasons for behaving in a particular way, and this understanding can then help you feel more relaxed and comfortable about that event.

> **CASE STUDY**
>
> Rick (aged forty) lived on an estate which housed many families with teenage children. As a consequence, there was a lot of noise and rowdy behaviour from the youngsters, particularly in summer when everyone spent time outdoors. The kids drove around on their bikes, jostled, fought and hung out in groups at the bottom of the stairwells leading up to the flats. Because of this, Rick felt very nervous when he walked across the estate on his way home from work. He felt that his reaction was over the top – after all, none of the youngsters had ever attacked him or even spoken to him – and yet, he felt quite panicky. This bothered him.

Rick's reaction was understandable, because groups of youths can feel very threatening, especially when they are noisy and boisterous. However, there is no need to go through the agony of prolonged anxiety and panic feelings. To tone down these fears, Rick did the following exercise.

Swapping places exercise

This mental exercise uses visualisation to help you gain a different perspective.

What to do

- Close your eyes and think of the situation that makes you feel uncomfortable. Think about it in as much detail as you can.

- Imagine yourself moving through this situation as you would in reality, and explore how you feel.

- Now run through the same situation, but step into the other person's shoes. As you are now moving around, acting and reacting, how do you feel as the other person? Why are you acting and reacting the way you do? How are you feeling about yourself? How are you feeling about that person you are looking at (namely, you)? Check carefully whether you are trying to impress them, impress others around you or whether you are masking an inner insecurity with your behaviour.

- Swap places again and be yourself once more. Now that you have experienced the other person's feelings, how does that change how *you* feel? How is this changing your perception of the situation?

In Rick's case, this meant having to step into the shoes of one of the teenagers. When he tried out being loud and obnoxious, he realised that he was trying to impress his friends and to be the same as them. Rick explored in his mind what it felt like to walk around with a swagger and discovered that it felt cool and macho. Once he had understood that the kids behaved as they did to show off rather than intentionally threaten him, his stress levels dropped and he felt much more comfortable walking across his estate.

How do I know I'm doing it right?
You should feel you have learnt something after the exercise, and that insight will help you adopt a more positive approach to the situation.

Troubleshooting
I simply cannot imagine why someone else would act like that. Please don't try and rationalise the exercise. It is *essential* you don't try to understand the other person *logically* but step into their shoes and *feel* what is going on within. Make sure you move like the other person and say (in your mind) their words in their tone of voice. All this will bring you more closely in touch with their feelings. You may be surprised to find that someone who talks aggressively actually feels frightened.

CHAPTER FOUR

Being true to your Self

In the previous chapters, we explored various ways in which we can deal with negative life patterns, free ourselves from negative self-beliefs and overcome past traumatic experiences. These are important concerns, which need to be addressed if you want to get back in touch with your Self and build a happy and fulfilled life.

So far, we have looked at issues that are connected to your background and experience. Now it is time to look at each individual aspect of your Self – body, mind, emotions and Soul – in order to access and heal each one of them.

Before you start working on these four aspects on an individual level, I would like you to take the time to evaluate how you interact with people around you. The first section of this chapter (see opposite) will help you assimilate the progress you made in Part 1 by applying your new-found confidence in your social environment.

Positive thinking is clearly beneficial for the individual, but its effects extend far beyond the confines of Self. Positive thinking creates a powerful positive energy field which, like a ripple on a lake, affects many people around the positive thinker in a beneficial way. Sometimes, however, difficult people can have a negative impact on your positive attitude, and it is important that you deal with them in a constructive way that allows you to stay focused and comfortable within yourself. In the following section we will be looking at ways of achieving this.

Next, we will be getting back in touch with the Self in more depth. In order to make positive changes in your life, you need to be able to tune in to what is going on in your body and mind, as well as start to make contact with the more spiritual side of your being. Once these connections are established, you can help yourself progress further by using your powers of imagination to shift thoughts and ideas into the right place in your mind. These mental visualisation exercises are then complemented by a number of healing movements that help the body to release old unwanted behaviour and thinking patterns that manifest on a physical level.

On page 149 we look in detail at how you can choose the right flower remedies for yourself and how to use either muscle testing or a pendulum to determine the right dosage.

To make sure that all your good work does not get undone by electro-magnetic disturbances, this is followed by a section that gives advice on how to combat noxious electro-magnetic fields and geopathic stress (see page 157). Next comes a section on rebalancing your energies in the face of general everyday stress (see page 168). In order to check your progress, the final section offers you an opportunity to check how far you have come on your path to finding your Self and becoming whole again. If you have not done so yet, go through the tests in the previous section (see pages 73, 84 and 98) and grade your answers. You will need this grading later to find out how much you have moved forward in your personal development.

Interacting positively with the world around you

We all know how one ill-tempered person in a family or in an office can ruin the atmosphere for everybody around them – all of us have experienced that at one time or another. It is as if the negative energy spreads from that person to everyone else in their environment. You can virtually 'catch' negativity from others like the common cold.

I remember one time going to give an interview on the radio. As I arrived, I was met by a man in the foyer who introduced himself by saying, 'My name is David Taylor, and everything is my fault.' I had no idea what this man was doing there or why he was saying everything was his fault. I felt very uncomfortable and didn't know how to respond to his statement. It later turned out that he was the producer of the programme. There had been some internal discord, and he offloaded his frustration on someone who had nothing to do with it – poor old me!

During the programme, I noticed how ill-at-ease the presenter seemed. I had worked with him before, and he had always been cheerful and bubbly, but not this time. He seemed a little quiet and subdued, and we got very few people calling in to the show. The producer's morose attitude seemed to spread to the end of the airwaves throughout the country!

But it is not just people around us who pick up on the vibes we send out. Even nature reacts to our thoughts! Dr Masaru Emoto, whose experiments with frozen water crystals were discussed earlier in the book, has conducted many other experiments with water. In 1997, he filled a cup with tap water from Shinagawa and placed it on the table in his office.

He took a photograph of a water crystal which revealed severe distortion and fragmentation in the crystal. He then contacted 500 of his graduates, asking them to send feelings of love to the water on a particular day at a particular time. He asked everyone to send their wishes for the water to become clean and healthy.

When Dr Emoto photographed the water after it had received all these positive energies from people all over Japan, the water was physically different and displayed symmetrical and harmonious crystal forms. He said that many of his staff were so moved when they saw this change that they were close to tears. The results of this experiment seem to indicate that positive energies can be pooled and transmitted over considerable distances to places where they are able to effect physical changes. It was not even necessary for the positive thinkers to be in the direct vicinity of the water.

The effects of positive thinking have a direct impact on how you feel physically and emotionally, and they will also influence your rate of performance. But just as the power of thought affects you, it also affects the people you spend time with, no matter how briefly. The producer who took me through to the studio was only in my presence for about five minutes, and yet he influenced my mood.

Of course, if you spend a lot of time with someone such as a family member or a colleague at work, they will have an even greater influence on your general well-being. This is why it is actually bad for your health to stay in a workplace or in a relationship with a negative atmosphere. Negative vibes drain your energy and stunt your potential.

Check what is going on in your head on a daily basis to ensure that it isn't *you* who is sapping other people's energy.

Exercise – what thoughts are ruling your life?

A practical exercise to find out what is going on in your head.

What to do

- Make a point of checking what sort of thoughts are going through your mind whenever you get the opportunity. Are the thoughts positive, negative or neutral/factual? Notice which category prevails.

- If you find yourself thinking mostly negatively, convert the thought into a positive or at least a factual one.

Examples

Negative: I'll never learn to do this job!

Neutral: This job seems very complicated.

Positive: This job seems complicated now, but I'm sure I will get the hang of it after a while.

Negative: I'm just not good-looking/young/attractive enough to ever find a partner.

Neutral: It is time I did something about my appearance/I

may not be perfect, but I'm making the best of my appearance. Positive: I want to make the best of my looks/I have made the best of my looks. I'm ready for a partner.

How long does it take?
Check what thoughts are going through your mind at least five times every day for a whole week.

What's the aim?
To become aware of whether you unwittingly drift off into negative thinking. To give yourself greater control over your thinking. Only when you *notice* that something is wrong can you set it right. To create positive energy within yourself and for people around you.

Bearing Dr Emoto's experiment in mind, make sure you focus positive thoughts on friends who are unhappy or ill. If your friend or a close family member suffers from a severe illness, it is only natural to be worried, and it would be very difficult to 'switch off' those worries altogether. And yet, you can make a conscious effort several times a day to send warm, loving thoughts of recovery to the other person so that the positive energies of your thoughts can bolster their energy levels. If you can get a few people together to do so at fixed times during the day, the impact can be multiplied. Praying does the same thing, only that with praying, the positive requests are routed via God. Worrying incessantly sends heavy energy. Sending positive thoughts conveys healing energies.

In order to send positive energy, you must be focused. Imagine a diffuse light shining on an object – the object will only be dimly lit. If you bundle the light into one clearly directed beam, more light will be concentrated on the object and it will be much more visible. In a similar way, it is necessary to have a very clear intention when sending positive thoughts to someone else. The same applies, of course, when you want positive thoughts to help yourself overcome a particular problem.

The following exercise will help you 'bundle' your positive thoughts in such a way that they become a powerful beam.

Exercise – spreading positive vibrations

This is a mental exercise that helps turn words into positive energy.

What to do

- Find a keyword for the feeling you want to send, either to yourself or to someone else. Be precise. Find the best possible word for what you want to send. Let's say your friend is depressed. Do you want to send 'joy' or 'hope', for example?

- Close your eyes and listen 'into' yourself.

- Think the keyword and allow the thought to take over your body and mind. Keep thinking the word with passion and notice what feelings begin to develop in your body. You are now creating the energy frequency that resonates with the word.

- Now imagine sending these thought vibrations to your friend. Remain with your eyes closed and imagine a wave of energy information travelling through the air to your friend.

- Keep this wave visualisation going for as long as you can.

How long does it take?
Two to three minutes.

What's the aim?
To transfer positive energy information to someone else. To support someone else's healing process. To feel encouraged yourself.

Troubleshooting
I can't decide on one keyword only. I have several that I feel are very important. That is fine. Just do one after the other.

I don't understand why it is so important to pick a particular word. The clearer your intention is, the more powerful the energy you send out. Vague thoughts get vague results.

We send out the vibrations of our own thoughts and we receive energy information from other people's thoughts. While it is essential to monitor your own thoughts, you need to be aware of outside sources that can influence you as well. Negative thoughtforms can come not only from other people, but also via the media. Both can have a detrimental impact on your energy field.

It can be tricky to deal with negativity when it comes from someone close to you, for example a parent or a good friend. A warning sign is when you feel down and depleted every time you speak to them in person or on the phone. When someone leaves you feeling physically weak and mentally drained, even though they are not saying anything particularly negative, check out the following:

Do they speak positively but with a negative undertone? You may well pick up negative vibes intuitively without knowing why. Your only sure way of confirming that your intuition is right is to check on several occasions how you feel after you have spoken to that person. If you constantly feel down or empty afterwards, your intuition can be relied on.

Tip Next time you speak to that person, mention that you felt that they weren't entirely happy when you spoke to them last. Ask specifically if everything is all right. Some people need a little prod before they come out with the real story.

Do they sound hopeless or defeated when they speak to you? Listening to someone else sounding hopeless may make you want to withdraw. You instinctively feel that a depressed mood could be contagious and might make you feel low.

Tip Let the other person know that they sound depressed. Bring the conversation around to active solutions. Ask what your friend is planning on doing to remedy their situation. If you know them well, make some suggestions yourself. Allow some time for them to implement changes. Next time you speak to them, ask specifically what they have done to resolve their problem. If they haven't done anything and clearly just want to moan, you need to tell them that you are not prepared to listen to their tale of woe again and again unless they are willing to do something about it. This may not go down well, but neither will it do your friend any good to talk themselves into a moaning frenzy every time they speak to you. You are doing them a greater favour by directing them towards a solution than by listening to their depressed talk.

Are they critical of everything and everyone? If someone is critical of everyone, they will soon be critical of you as well.

Tip Be careful not to be drawn into gossiping about others, just because your friend feels the need to do so. It takes a lot of courage to oppose someone who gossips because most people are afraid that they will be at the receiving end of criticism if they don't fall in with the gossiper.

Be clear as well that someone who criticises others will automatically also talk critically about *you* behind your back. You might as well give them a real reason to be critical of you by telling them that you don't like listening to gossip. It is also perfectly okay to let them know that you don't agree with their criticism of the other person. This may not go down well, but if you lose this friend, you will also lose their negative vibes and that is good for you. Remember: great minds discuss ideas, average minds discuss events and small minds discuss people.

Do they tell you that you are the only one who understands them and everyone else is useless and uncaring? Beware! You are being made into the 'saviour' which may be flattering but brings with it great obligations which may soon weigh you down.

Tip Do not lose sight of the fact that you cannot save anyone. Everyone is responsible for their own well-being, you for yours and they for theirs. This does not mean that you should not lend a hand or a shoulder to cry on, but this can never be the only solution to their problems. Do help, but ultimately, it is up to them to do something to help themselves.

Do they only ever talk about themselves or others and never ask you how you are? Endless listening is tiring. A conversation needs to be a two-way process or it becomes an ordeal. Being talked at non-stop saps your energy – it makes you annoyed, uncomfortable and generally throws your energy out of balance. As a result, not only do *you* feel unsettled, but you also send out negative vibes to others – so the negative vibes start to multiply!

Tip This is about your boundaries. If you are bothered by someone who keeps talking about themselves, deal with the situation in a straightforward way. If you can't get a word in edgeways, sit back and break off eye contact. Stop reacting to what the other person says; stop nodding or changing your facial expression in response to the other person's monologue. Start looking around the room and notice whether the other person reacts. If you get 'Am I boring you/talking too much?', resume eye contact and say, 'You have been talking non-stop since we sat down. I find that tiring.' *Be honest!*

If the person continues talking while you are clearly not paying attention, pick up a paper or magazine and start leafing through it. If they ask, 'Am I boring you/talking too much?', give the same answer. *Be honest!*

If they still don't react, get up without a word and walk towards the door. If they react, give the same answer. If they continue talking and start following you, keep walking out of the front door and don't go back unless they ask you, 'Was I boring you/talking too much?' and you have given them your answer as above. If they never react, they are a health and energy hazard and you are better off away from them.

Are they always very intense and emotional when they speak to you? If a person is going through a crisis, it is very understandable that they should be emotional when they talk about their problems. That is okay and quite normal, although it can be wearing. On the other hand, it is the stuff friendship is made of to be there in a crisis and help a friend carry their burden part of the way.

Tip Do give your friend time to talk about their problems, but make sure you also distract them every once in a while. This gives both you and them time to recover a little from the emotional onslaught, even if it is only for five or ten minutes.

Tuning in to your inner world

Just as it is important to be sensitive to what is going on around us, so it is essential to be in touch with what is going on inside us. In many ways, we live from the inside out. Our personal experiences, our personality type, inclinations and coping mechanisms determine the way we look at life around us. We will act in the world according to our view of the world. Our behaviour towards the people around us depends upon our opinion of them.

This means that we need to be aware of our inner world in order to understand why we are successful or unsuccessful in our relationships or our professional aspirations, and why we experience emotional stability or instability.

Getting in touch with your inner world must, by necessity, cover *all* aspects that make up your unique being. It is not enough to just look at psychological issues such as the mind and the emotions. The mind and the emotions do not exist in a vacuum.

If I can develop a phobia when I am put on certain pharmaceutical drugs or when I eat a food that I'm allergic to, I need to make this connection or I can spend a small fortune going to psychotherapy sessions without getting the desired results. So even though you may want to sort out an emotional block with the help of this book, I would like you to do all the exercises and tests, be they for the mind, the body or the Soul. All four aspects will play together to make you whole again so you can find inner harmony and happiness.

Exercise for connecting with your physical side

This mental exercise focuses on the body, using visualisation to spread comfortable vibrations around the body.

What to do

- Loosen any tight clothing and lie down, legs stretched out, arms along your body. Put rolled up towels or a cushion under your head and behind your knees, if that makes you feel more comfortable.

■ Let your eyes close and listen to your breathing. Allow your breathing to go any way it wants to go and just listen to it. Feel how your chest and stomach area rise and fall gently with your breathing.

■ Be aware of any areas in your body that feel *comfortable*. Focus your inner attention on each of these comfortable areas in turn.

■ Imagine spreading these comfortable feelings throughout your body.

■ Now be aware of any areas in your body that are the *right temperature* – not too hot, not too cold. Focus on each of these areas in turn.

■ Imagine spreading the comfortable temperature throughout your body.

■ Now be aware of any areas in your body where you can feel a *pulse* beating. Focus on each of these areas in turn.

■ Imagine feeling this life-giving pulse in every part of your body, in every muscle, gland, organ and fibre, and in every single cell of your body. Be aware that you are now feeling life force pulsing through you.

How long does it take?

Do each of these steps – comfortable feeling, right temperature and pulse – for as long as you can concentrate on it. When you feel your attention wandering off, move on to the next step. Initially, you may find it hard to keep focused, so the exercise will be very short. As you practise more, your concentration will improve and the exercise will take a little longer, with clearer results.

What's the aim?

To become aware of your body, to relax and to start appreciating that your thoughts, once channelled, can have an influence on your body. To start listening to the messages your body gives you and to spread positive messages through your body. This basic exercise will help you identify physical symptoms early on, which is essential if you want to heal the body.

How do I know I'm doing it right?

When you feel calm and relaxed at the end, and particularly when you have been able to spread comfortable sensations around the body.

What to avoid

Telling yourself off if you can't concentrate. Just move on to the next part of the exercise and focus your mind on the next sensation.

Troubleshooting

I suffer from chronic pain and find it difficult to concentrate on the comfortable feelings. My mind is constantly drawn to the painful area. Acknowledge the pain, then move over to a comfortable site in your body. Say to yourself, 'I acknowledge this pain and at the same time I can also be aware of the comfortable area in my [name the area, for example 'leg'].'

I can feel all the sensations – comfort, warmth and pulse beating – but I cannot spread them to the rest of the body. Focus your attention on one part of the body where you *cannot* feel the sensation. Now speculate in your mind what it would feel like if you *could* experience the sensation there. Or you can pretend that the sensation is occurring, and as you do so you will notice that shortly afterwards, it actually does.

Tuning in to your emotions

Just as the body gives off signals, so do our emotions. Emotions can be a powerful inner driving force that determines our actions and reactions, our health, our mental stability and our ability to deal with stress. Emotions can become very apparent when they run high. When you are really happy or very angry, it will show in your posture, your gestures and your facial expression. At that point in time, we are clearly aware of our emotions, and so are others. But more often than not, feelings can be subconscious undercurrents that are not necessarily perceived very clearly. We may feel somewhat fed up, irritable or listless without being able to put a finger on the reason or the exact nature of our unease.

In sessions with clients, I have noticed that many feel they should not have certain feelings they have been brought up to believe to be undesirable or 'wrong', such as envy, jealousy, anger, sadness, desire and lust. But feelings are relative. If a two-year-old is moved out of his parents' bedroom because a new baby arrives, his feeling of jealousy is understandable. If, however, a wife goes through her husband's pockets when he gives her no reason to suspect him of having an affair, her jealousy is more difficult to understand.

All feelings are valid as they are part of being human, but if we are troubled by feelings that make us unhappy, we need to take action. Equally, if we are not able to enjoy any of the feel-good emotions such as love and happiness, it is our responsibility towards ourselves to work on changing this. After all, if you are not happy yourself, you can't make anyone else happy. Working on inner emotional happiness is good for you *and* everyone around you!

In the next exercise, I would like you to explore your feelings, be they 'good' or 'bad'. This simple exercise will help you recognise what feelings you have and what they feel like. Once you can name and recognise a feeling, it becomes easier to identify it when you get it again.

Exercise for connecting with your emotional side

This mental exercise allows you to access your emotions and explore how they are reflected in physical feelings.

What to do

- Sit or lie down and place both hands on your navel. Listen in to yourself. What emotion can you detect? Is there only one particular emotion, or can you make out a number of different ones? Are your emotions mixed – that is, contra-dictory – for example happiness and fear, satisfaction and neediness? Or are they of the same kind, such as fear and loathing, happiness and contentment, loneliness and rejection?

- Identify each emotion separately. Let's say you discovered fear inside yourself. Notice where in your body the fear is located. Do you feel it in your head, in your stomach area or anywhere else? What happens to your breathing while you feel the fear? Is there a change in your body temperature? Notice as much detail as you can.

- Acknowledge the fear by addressing it with the thought, 'You are my fear. You are part of me and I resist you no longer.' Do the same with every single emotion.

How long does it take?

Take your time over this exercise. Don't rush it, but really listen in to yourself very carefully. The more feelings you can find and acknowledge, the more complete will be your inner picture of who you are. When you can find only positive emotions, you need not do this exercise again until you feel the need to. If you have mostly negative emotions, do the exercise every day.

What's the aim?

To become connected to all your emotions and, by accepting the positive ones, make them stronger, and by accepting the negative ones, make them less frightening and less over-powering.

How do I know I'm doing it right?

It is a good sign when you can stay calm and accepting while thinking about a negative emotion. Also, when you feel more appreciative and happy about positive ones, it tells you that you have gained from the exercise.

What to avoid
Cheating. Please do not ignore negative emotions, just because you feel they should not be there. Not looking at them won't make them go away.

Troubleshooting
The moment I start looking for any emotions, they all seem to disappear, and that annoys me. There you are! Here's your emotion – annoyance. Work with that. Or if you feel disappointed because you can't find any emotions, work with 'disappointment'.

I only seem to ever feel negative emotions. Am I doing something wrong or am I just a hopeless case? No, you are a very promising case. You can admire your own thoroughness when it comes to negative emotions, so do the exercise again, this time working with 'admiration' (for your persistence) and 'devotion' (to your negative thoughts).

Tip Make sure you do not confuse an emotional feeling with a physical condition that is brought on by foods or stimulants. Fear can give you butterflies in your stomach, but so can too much tea or coffee! Certain pharmaceutical or recreational drugs can make you feel lethargic, dizzy or anxious. Also, not eating enough can make you feel weak, light-headed and fearful.

Tuning in to your spirit

So now that you have explored the physical and emotional side of your Self, try out what it feels like to get in touch with your spiritual side. If you are quite used to doing meditation or yoga, you will already have a good grasp of what it feels like to be centred and grounded while at the same time linking up with the greater picture around you. For those of you who have so far regarded spirits as something you find on the shelf of your local off-licence, have a go anyway! Consider the next exercise an experiment which may or may not be right for you. You are not meddling with anything dangerous – the exercise is simply a way of expanding your awareness.

Exercise for connecting with your spiritual side

This meditation exercise allows you to access the spiritual level of your Self.

What to do

- With your eyes closed, imagine yourself somewhere outdoors. Make this a landscape that allows you to look far into the distance, such as the top of a mountain or the sea shore. Your surroundings should symbolise peace and tranquillity for you.

- In your imagination, remain with this image until you can feel yourself getting calm and peaceful inside.

- Imagine that you begin to see a veil of mist on the horizon which separates you from the spiritual side of life.

- Watch the veil slowly moving closer to you and feel your happy anticipation at soon coming into contact with the home of your Soul.

- When the veil is right in front of you, reach with both hands through the mist to greet the spiritual part of yourself, welcoming it into your life. You can either reach out your hands physically or just imagine doing so.

- Now wait and see what happens.

Some people experience a tingling or warmth in their hands, others feel very happy at the thought of connecting with a higher dimension which makes them feel less alone. At times, people also find themselves connecting up with loved ones who have passed away, and this can be very comforting.

How long does it take?

As long as you like. You can do this exercise every day if you want to, but remember that, in itself, it will not change your life if you do not do all the practical things that are necessary to improve your situation.

What's the aim?

To get in touch with your spiritual side. To create a feeling that you belong to something greater than your immediate physical environment.

How do I know I'm doing it right?

A good sign is when you feel a positive emotion such as happiness, deep inner peace or a sense of homecoming or belonging. Remember that this exercise, like all the other exercises in this book, will be an entirely subjective, personal experience. There is no right or wrong, there is only *your* experience.

What to avoid

Wanting to force an experience or a particular outcome. The more open-minded you remain, the more likely it is that you will gain from this exercise.

Troubleshooting

I can't get a calm and peaceful feeling when I'm standing in my landscape. See if you can remember one time in your life when you felt calm. Remember that time, together with the peaceful feeling, and then bring the feeling with you into your landscape.

I can't see a veil of mist. It doesn't have to be a veil of mist. You can also imagine a curtain. Look at a curtain you have in your house and use this as an aid for your imagination.

I'm not getting anything when I reach out my hands, only feelings of disappointment. Make sure you do not overlook what is actually happening. If you are too busy focusing on a preconceived idea of how it *should* be, you will miss out on what actually *is*. If you feel your mind is genuinely open but nothing happens, add the following thought as you reach through the veil, 'I now connect with the home of my Soul and receive with thanks any feelings that show me I'm connected.' Keep repeating the exercise daily and pay attention to the feelings you get when you reach through the veil.

Positive visualisation

Have you ever watched someone dreaming while they are asleep? You can see their eyeballs moving behind the closed lids, and sometimes they will even murmur some words or move their arms and legs. The dream, which runs like a film through the mind, activates the body. This dreaming response can also be observed in cats and dogs when they are sleeping.

As there is such a strong link between body and mind, it makes sense to use this connection for healing purposes. Visualisation is an excellent self-help method which you can employ anywhere, anytime. The only condition is that you need to be able to close your eyes, so doing it while driving a car or working machinery is definitely out!

There is no need for lengthy periods of relaxation before visualisation exercises except when you are dealing with a strong fear. In this case it makes sense to do the psoas exercise (see page 76) or the collarbone breathing (see page 88) first, to get your tension level down and feel more grounded. Once you are more relaxed, you can then go immediately into your visualisation exercise.

The nice thing about visualisation is that you don't have to do it perfectly for it to work. Seeing with your eyes closed can be very different to seeing with your eyes open. Try it out:

- Look at an object in the room, for example a telephone, a chair or a plant. Look at the object in great detail.

- Now close your eyes and imagine the same object. How is your perception of the object different now?

When you 'see' something in your imagination, you may:

- Not see any colour.

- Not get a sharply defined picture.

- Not get a picture at all but merely an idea of what the object probably looks like.

- Not be able to hold the picture in your mind.

It doesn't matter! You will still get results. If you can't stop criticising yourself for not visualising accurately enough, go back to page 120 and do the exercise 'Connecting with your emotional side' and work with 'self-criticism'.

In the following exercises, we will be using positive visualisation techniques on all three levels: physical, emotional and spiritual. By now, you will have got in touch with these different levels of your Self; now the healing process can truly begin.

For the body

You may find it peculiar that you are asked to do a visualisation exercise for your body even though you may not have any physical problems. But don't forget that even though it may be your emotions that are giving you problems, the body will be affected as well. The body 'holds' memories of events and emotions, even if you are not always aware of it.

This is why smokers often find it so difficult to give up: their bodies remember that a phone call goes with a cigarette/the end of a meal/a glass of beer. If you have ever smoked you will know how your hand automatically reaches for the cigarettes when you are in a situation which, for you personally, is subconsciously associated with smoking. This phenomenon is called 'muscle memory'.

So even though your main problem may be low self-esteem, this will be reflected in the way you hold yourself, your breathing, your posture and your muscle tension. If you can give your body a break so it can let go of at least *some* of this tension, this will have a beneficial effect on your emotions as well.

Exercise for healing the body

This mental exercise uses visualisation to promote physical well-being.

What to do

- Loosen tight clothing. Sit or lie down and close your eyes.

- Listen to your breathing and feel the movement of your body as it expands and deflates with your breathing.

- Imagine that any physical tension now starts draining out of your body via your fingertips and your toes.

- Concentrate on the centre of your body.

- While you concentrate, imagine a sun being located in the centre of your stomach area, radiating warmth and strength outwards into the upper body, arms and head and into the lower body, legs and feet.

- Now imagine sparkling particles like fireworks spreading among the pathways that the rays of sunshine are making through the body, filling every muscle and fibre and cell with energy.

- If you know that there is a problem with a particular organ or gland, shift the sun over to that area so that this organ is receiving the full impact of the warmth, strength and energy of the sun and the sparkling particles. Hold this image as long as you can.

How long does it take?

Spin this exercise out as long as you can to get maximum benefit from it. Repeat it regularly, especially if you suffer from an illness or if you feel emotionally vulnerable.

What's the aim?

To release tension from the body. To promote healing, both physically and emotionally. To raise energy levels and make you more stress-resilient.

How do I know I'm doing it right?

You feel calmer and physically more relaxed and refreshed. You may even fall asleep, so this is a particularly good exercise to do when you are having problems getting to sleep.

What to avoid

Rushing through the exercise.

Troubleshooting

I can't see a sun. If you can imagine what the sun probably looks like, that will do. Or you could concentrate more on the tactile sensations. What would it feel like if you had a sun in the centre of your body? What would it feel like if those sparkling particles rushed through your body?

I just can't lie still long enough to do this exercise properly. Do the exercise improperly then. Do it standing up while you are leaning against the wall. It would also be useful if you did the emotion exercise for 'impatience' (see page 120).

For the emotions

With the body in a more relaxed state, you can now go on to give some attention to your emotions. In the previous chapter, you have worked at recognising and acknowledging your feelings. Now, I would like to take you one step further. In order to heal your emotions, you need to recognise that they all serve a beneficial purpose. In the next exercise, you will be asked to spend some time finding out what this purpose is and to renegotiate a better deal for yourself. Sounds weird, but it works!

Exercise for healing negative emotions

This mental exercise uses visualisation to access and heal limiting emotions.

What to do

- Sit or lie down comfortably and place your hands on your navel. Close your eyes.

- Allow a negative emotion to come forward within you and name it by thinking 'This is my [anger/envy/…].'

- Imagine you could take the emotion out of yourself and place it in front of you as a person. What would your personified emotion look like? Would it be a man or a woman? Is it someone you know or someone you have never seen before?

- Watch the personified emotion express that feeling. Watch them rant and rave in anger, sit with head in hands with depression, or do whatever expresses the emotion they are representing.

- Address the person in your mind with the following words, 'You have a very special part in my life and I don't know what I'd do without you. You are very important to me.' Check how you feel.

- Now swap places and be the personified emotion. *Feel* the anger, depression or whatever else you are representing. Feel yourself acting and expressing that feeling physically, either through words or by your posture and body tension. Now hear the words that are addressed to you, 'You have a very special part in my life and I don't know what I'd do without you. You are very important to me.' Check how you feel as the personified emotion who hears these words.

- Swap places again and reintegrate the personified emotion back into you. See how it feels different now. Open your eyes again.

How long does it take?
Unimportant. Take your time.

What's the aim?
To acknowledge and honour a negative feeling. It is there for a reason and has probably served as a useful self-preservation mechanism in the past. By conveying your respect for it, the negative feeling can abate. Trying to sweep a negative feeling under the carpet gives it power over you; facing it and acknowledging it gives you the power to deal with it.

How do I know I'm doing it right?
At the end of the exercise you will feel more peaceful inside.

What to avoid
Working with too many negative emotions in one go. Allow the effects of the exercise to percolate through your body and mind for a day and leave tackling the next emotion to the next day. Less is more.

Troubleshooting
I can't see the personified emotion clearly in my mind. It doesn't matter. If you can imagine what the person would look like if you could see them, that will do.

I feel really embarrassed saying these words to the personified emotion. That's okay. Do another round tomorrow on 'embarrassment'.

When I'm stepping into the personified emotion's shoes, I get carried away with expressing the emotion and can't really concentrate on hearing the words said to me. Turn up the volume of the words in your mind!

For the spirit

In order to complete the picture, we need the spiritual dimension in our visualisation cycle. Feeling that you are part of a dimension countless times more vast than your immediate environment creates a sense of belonging that is independent of who you are, what you are and who you are with. Especially if you feel lonely, abandoned or rejected, the following exercise can give great comfort and relief.

Exercise for connecting to heaven and Earth

This mental exercise allows you to make a physical and mental link between your body and your extended environment, helping to develop your spiritual side.

What to do

- Make yourself comfortable and close your eyes.

- Be aware of how your back connects with the chair, or mattress if you are lying down. Be aware of the air that is touching your face and hands, and be aware of the space above your body.

- Imagine yourself connecting downwards with your spine, through the floor into the ground on which the building stands. Imagine connecting even further down into the earth below the building, and further down right into the core of the Earth, linking you with the forces of nature that reside deep within the Earth.

- Now concentrate on the space above your body, the empty space up to the ceiling, and begin to link up with that space above you. Imagine the space above you is an extension of your body, and now take that extension higher and further out – into the sky, past the clouds, into the upper stratosphere that is surrounding the Earth, right out into space.

- As you are feeling the connections down into the Earth and up into the universe, say to yourself, 'I am one with the Earth and the sky. Mother Earth and Father Sky carry me safely always.'

How long does it take?

You can do this exercise relatively quickly once you have practised it a bit. It does not necessarily get better the longer you do
it. The main point is to feel 'connected'.

Aim

To experience a sense of belonging and oneness with nature
and the universe.

How do I know I'm doing it right?

As soon as you can feel a physical or emotional 'link' down
into the Earth and up into space, you know that you have
achieved the objective of this exercise. The 'link' can feel like a
sigh or an opening of the stomach area, or it can be an
emotional feeling of relief or satisfaction.

Avoid

Prejudging what the 'link' will feel like. Observe what happens
and accept it as *your* way of linking.

Troubleshooting

This exercise is too abstract for me. Imagine Mother Earth is
your bed and Father Sky is your blanket. Together, they take
care of you – Mother Earth holds and supports you and Father
Sky soothes you.

This exercise is too far out for me. That is fine. You don't
have to like everything in this book. Just leave out this exercise and use those that feel more 'normal' to you. You may
want to come back to it at a later stage. It may be too early
for you to do this exercise, so it is better to leave it for the
time being.

Future projection

In the last three exercises, you have focused on particular areas
of your Self. In order to pull all the previous work together, it

is good to do a future projection exercise. This is a bit like getting into a time machine that takes you forward to where you want to be, to a time where you have achieved your aim and where you feel whole again.

It is okay to let your imagination run free whilst doing this exercise. Dare to imagine the best outcome for yourself! A word of warning, however: if you do this exercise regularly but do not follow on with constructive action in real life, your goal will remain a pipe dream. Success is always a combination of positive attitude and constructive action.

Exercise for a happy ending

This mental exercise uses visualisation to help you focus on a positive outcome.

What to do

- Sit or lie down comfortably and close your eyes.

- Imagine standing in front of a full-length mirror and see your reflection in the mirror.

- As you are looking at your reflection, imagine a soft grey mist beginning to fill the mirror until it has obscured your reflection entirely.

- Take a deep breath and step into the mirror. You are safe and secure as the soft grey mists carry you gently forward in time to that day when you have overcome the particular problem you are working on now.

- Imagine yourself being set down by the mists on that happy day and watch them clear around you. Notice in detail how your life is different now that you have overcome the problem. Feel all the happy feelings that go with having achieved your aim. Notice all the things you are able to do which you couldn't do before. Feel what it is like to do all these things now. Enjoy the elation. Stay in that feeling for a while.

- Now let the soft grey mists surround you again and carry you gently backwards in time, until you step backwards out of the mirror.

- Watch the mists clear from the mirror until you can see your own reflection again.

- Take a piece of chalk and write across the mirror, *'This is how it will be!'*

- Open your eyes again.

How long does it take?
Spin this one out, especially your happy feelings when you imagine you have achieved your aim. Do this exercise daily.

What's the aim?
To stay focused on your aim. To stay motivated and optimistic.

How do I know I'm doing it right?
A clear sign is when you feel uplifted at the end of the exercise.

Troubleshooting
I can't really see where I am or what I'm doing once I've arrived at that future day. You can simply make up what you want to see and do if that makes things easier for you. It will still work.

I feel I'm kidding myself by doing this exercise. After all, I haven't achieved my aim yet! You are not kidding yourself – you are encouraging yourself and strengthening your resolve. Staying focused on an aim makes it more likely that you will succeed.

Healing movements

If you have ever had a massage, you will know how good you feel afterwards. The sensation of someone shifting and moving the muscles under your skin has a healing effect not just on your body but also on your mind. For a while after the massage, you feel calm, relaxed and comfortably tired.

But it is not just the massaging movements, but also the skin-to-skin contact that is important. One problem with being on your own is that often you do not have enough skin contact. We know today how important it is that a new-born baby is placed in the mother's arms or, even better, directly on her belly immediately after birth, as the direct skin contact is soothing and comforting.

By touching the skin, we can rebalance body, mind and spirit. The next exercise gives you a simple and effective way of chilling out, relaxing the body and thereby regaining your emotional equilibrium.

During the exercise, you will be stroking your neurovascular (NV) reflex points which are located on the forehead, directly above the centre of each eye. These NV points were discovered in the early 1930s by Dr Terence Bennett, a Californian chiropractor.

Dr Bennett found that touching these points lightly sent a signal through the nervous system to increase supply to various tissues in the body where the flow had been blocked. He validated his idea by holding the NV points and watching the changes in blood flow through a fluorscope, which is a fluorescent screen that shows up images of internal organs in motion.

As blood circulates through the body, it provides all the tissues with nutrients and energy. Arteries carry oxygenated blood away from the heart to all parts of the body. The arteries branch out into smaller and smaller blood vessels until the blood flows through minute capillaries that serve specific tissues. In times of stress, be it physical exertion or emotional upheaval, those tissues that are not necessary for physical survival, such as the higher cortical areas of the brain, the skin and the digestive organs, are deprived of full blood supply. Only capillaries in the tissues necessary for immediate survival, for example muscles and the more primitive parts of the brain, receive full supply.

By doing the next exercise, you are activating the NV points on your forehead to open up blood supply to *all* the tissues in your body.

Exercise for soothing the body and the mind

This energy technique works on the body's vibrational level to help relax body, mind and emotions.

What to do

- Rest both your middle fingers on the bridge of your nose, one finger next to the other.

- Open your eyes wide, looking very slightly upwards. Make sure you do not furrow your brow, though.

- Slowly and gently move your middle fingers up and then outwards towards your temples, all the way down to your ears. *Glide* your fingers over the skin surface. Do not press. Make sure you breathe while doing the exercise.

- Repeat this ten times.

- Now close your eyes and repeat the same finger movements across your forehead and down to your ears another ten times.

Moving the fingers from the bridge of the nose up and outwards to the temples.

How long does it take?
Take your time. Do this slowly.

What's the aim?
To relax, destress and feel centred and strong emotionally.

How do I know I'm doing it right?
You will feel your forehead relax, together with your jaw muscles. You may also notice that you are breathing more deeply during or after the exercise. A yawn is also a good sign.

The role of the meridians

It is not only through direct touch that healing movements become effective. Just by moving your hands over the body at a distance of 1 or 2 inches can you achieve excellent results. To understand why this is so, we need to look again briefly at the pathways that carry life force through the body – the meridians.

There are fourteen meridians in total, which run skin-deep through the body. The width of each meridian is about the same as the diameter of a single cell. Meridians are electro-magnetic by nature. The flow of energy in the meridians can be disturbed by imbalances in any aspect of life: emotions, thoughts, relationships, chemicals, electro-magnetic pollution, nutrition, and so on.

When we are stressed, emotionally or physically through illness, the energy can no longer flow freely through the meridians; there is suddenly a subtle energy block. Initially, we can still function normally, but if the stress continues, more blocks appear, less energy gets to the relevant tissues in the body, and we start feeling that we are no longer firing on all cylinders.

Two meridians are particularly important. These are the Governing Vessel (GV) which runs up your spine, over your head and ends just under your nose above your upper lip. The GV governs the spine. The other meridian is the Central Vessel (CV) which runs up the midline of your body and ends under your lower lip. The CV governs your brain. It is the CV that we will work with in the next exercise.

Even though meridians run under the skin, their energy extends approximately 2 inches outside the body. To sense the meridians:

- Hold your hand about a foot away from the trunk of your body, with the palm towards the body.

- Bring the palm of your hand very slowly closer to your body and be aware of the feelings in your hand.

- Notice at what point you can feel the closeness of your body without actually touching it.

Depending on how sensitive you are, you will be able to feel warmth or a pulse coming from your body quite early on. If you can feel your body with your hand even though you are not touching it, your body can feel your hand as well. You do not actually have to touch your body to enter its energy field.

The CV runs from below to above. If it is blocked it needs to be 'turned on' again, and this is what is called 'zipping up' in kinesiology.

Zip up exercise

This energy exercise helps to activate the meridian that runs your brain.

What to do

- Stand up and place both hands, one on top of the other, over the area of your pubic bone.

- Run both hands, one on top of the other, up the midline of your body and neck. Trace its path up to the chin below the lower lip. Stop here.

- Take your hands out to the side, arms stretched away from the body, then let them gently drop down to your side.

- Repeat ten times.

How long does it take?

Approximately one minute. A good time to do this exercise is first thing in the morning.

What's the aim?

To switch on the Central Vessel (CV) that governs the brain. This will help the brain to work more easily and efficiently. This is important because the brain is the control centre for all physical and emotional functions.

How do I know I'm doing it right?

You feel your breathing getting deeper and you feel more together. Ideal when you are stressed or anxious.

Tips

- Don't dawdle when you are zipping up your CV. Do it just a little slower than zipping up a long jacket.

- It doesn't matter whether you breathe in or out while you are zipping up. Let your breath find its own preferred rhythm.

The zip up exercise works on your body via the CV. As you switch on the CV, this will have an effect on both your physical and mental state by allowing the brain to work at full force while at the same time balancing the body.

The next exercise also works primarily on the body, but you will be required to link in your thoughts with the Earth and with the universe around you. This means that, again, you are working on several levels – by moving the body and employing thought processes, you are accessing the spiritual side of your Self.

Mother Earth and Father Sky exercise

This energy technique will help to make you feel more grounded and, at the same time, more connected with your spiritual side.

What to do

- Stand with your feet hip-width apart, hands by your side. Look straight ahead.

- Shift your weight on to one foot and push the arm on that side down towards the floor a little. Think: 'Mother Earth'.

- Shift your weight on to the other foot and push the other arm down towards the floor a little. Think: 'Mother Earth'.

- Sway from side to side like this ten times.

- Now raise your arms up and look upwards. Continue swaying from one foot to the other and, as your weight is on the left foot, raise the left hand towards the sky, then with the weight on the right foot, raise the right hand to the sky, thinking each time 'Father Sky'.

- Sway from side to side like this ten times.

How long does it take?

Approximately one minute.

What's the aim?

To allow your body to gather energies coming from the Earth and the sky. This strengthens your intuitive understanding that you are linked to both heaven and to Earth, giving you a sense of belonging.

How do I know I'm doing it right?

A good sign is if you get an involuntary deep breath during or after the exercise. You may also find yourself feeling uplifted afterwards.

Tips

- Do this exercise with concentration and purpose. Be aware of every movement you make.

- Do not strain whilst doing any of the movements.

- Keep breathing.

- If you are ill and cannot stand up, do the exercise sitting down and simply sway from side to side. If you cannot move your feet or raise your arms, use the direction of your gaze to help you focus on what you are connecting with. Eyes straight ahead connects with the surface of the Earth, eyes upwards connects with the sky.

The wisdom of nature

Imagine you live in a remote village without technology where people love music. In every house there is at least one person who plays an instrument. During weekday evenings, music drifts from the open windows of the houses as the musicians are practising on their own, or in little groups, and at weekends the village orchestra gives concerts.

One day, a man comes to your village to listen to the orchestra playing. After the concert, he produces a little black box and claims that he has captured the music in the box. He opens the lid and takes out a small case, which contains a brown tape. He shows it to you and the other villagers and tells you that this is where the music is stored.

The villagers, including yourself, find this statement confusing. How can an entire orchestra be in this little case? This is clearly impossible. The man explains to you that he has captured the sound of the music in all its detail on the brown tape. Now you know for sure that he is a fraud. How can you capture a sound that drifts through the air and is gone as soon as it has been played? How can sound stick to a tape? Logic and simple common sense tell you that this is impossible.

Now the man produces a cord with two little buttons at the end and invites you to put them to your ears and listen. He places the little case back in the black box and presses a button. You cannot believe your ears, but there it is – you can hear the orchestra playing, just as it did a moment ago, and the sound comes from the little black box. Every villager in turn listens to the music, and they all agree: this is some sort of trick, or the stranger is in league with the devil. In either case, nobody wants him and he is asked to leave the village. But for weeks after, people discuss the implausibility of capturing something that is invisible on a little brown tape in a box.

When I tell people about my work as a health kinesiologist, I often encounter this 'village' attitude: how can you test an arm muscle response, hold a few acupuncture points or place magnets on the body and claim that this will make your hair grow back or your duodenal ulcers disappear? Equally, how can a homeopath prescribe an essence that is diluted to such an extent that there is no measurable trace of the original substance left? How can anyone be sure that they are taking anything that is really there? The answer is that, both in kinesiology and in homeopathy, we are working at a subtle energy level.

Normally, we experience our physical body through our senses of sight, touch, sound, taste and smell. We know that the body is made out of skin, bones, muscles, lymph, blood and so on, but over and above the visible components, there are subtle energy systems at work. These energy systems are electrical and, just like electricity, cannot be seen unless you use electrophotography, which will show up a corona of electrical discharge around the human body. This electrophotography was carried out as early as the 1940s by Harold S. Burr at Yale University and Semyon Kirlian, a Russian researcher.

Subtle energies play a major role in the smooth functioning of the body. As they flow through it, they influence not only all our glands and organs, but also our muscles. When subtle energy is blocked, this block will weaken a muscle. The same weakness will occur when we bring an allergenic food near the body, when we think a negative thought, or when we touch a bottle of inappropriate flower essence.

When energy flows freely and the body is in balance, the muscles will be well toned and strong. The same strength response will occur when a beneficial food is brought near the body, when we think positive thoughts or when we touch a bottle of appropriate flower essence. The body is able, via the subtle energy system, to tell us what we need and what is not suitable or even harmful for us.

One way of using a muscle to give us information about the suitability of a substance is through muscle testing. The muscle will respond powerfully when it picks up the right vibrational pattern of a remedy that is beneficial for you at that point in time.

In the following pages, I will introduce two types of muscle testing. One works by you using your fingers, the other one involves a simple pendulum. The finger muscle testing is useful because you always have your test apparatus on you, and it is also less conspicuous than the pendulum. I would like you to practise both methods, however, because the pendulum can come in handy when you can sit down and choose from a written list of remedies.

Finger testing exercise

This energy technique teaches you to use a muscle response as a biofeedback mechanism.

What to do

- Form a circle with your fingers by holding the tips of your right thumb and your right index finger together.

- Now form another circle like that with your left thumb and index finger which interlinks with the circle made by your right-hand fingers (see illustration, page 144).

- Set up a 'yes' and a 'no' response. While holding the fingers of each circle interlocked, say 'yes' in a determined way. Then pull the finger circles gently but firmly in opposite directions, away from one another, but keep the fingers locked so the circles stay together.

- Now say 'no', and pull the finger circles gently but firmly in opposite directions, away from one another. This time allow the finger circle of your dominant hand (the one you write with) to come apart so that the finger circles separate.

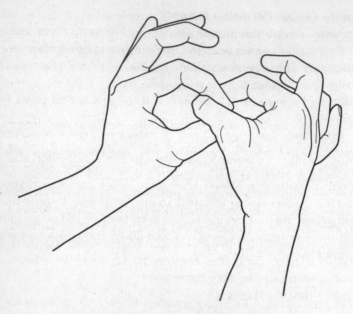

The fingers form two interlinked circles.

- Repeat the 'yes' and 'no' responses quickly in random fashion. Say 'yes', 'yes', 'no', 'no', 'no', 'no', 'yes' for example, and make sure you keep your fingers together or let them separate as appropriate. This is a way of training the brain to respond reliably to the words 'yes' and 'no' with the correct muscle action.

How long does it take?

This exercise itself takes seconds to do. However, to become good at it and to get reliable test results, it takes a lot of regular practice.

What's the aim?

To get a reliable 'yes' and 'no' response from the muscles of your fingers so that this response can later be used to determine which remedy or flower essence is appropriate for you to take.

How do I know I'm doing it right?

When you can do the muscle testing quickly, saying 'yes' and 'no' in random succession and the fingers stay together or come apart accurately every time.

Tips

- If you are having problems with the 'yes' and 'no' finger responses, replace the 'yes' with a statement that is clearly true. I could, for example, say 'My name is Vera Peiffer' and the finger circles stay together. If I then said 'My name is Mickey Mouse', the fingers would come apart. You can also use general statements such as 'It is sunny outside' whilst, in reality, it is dark (fingers come apart) or 'I live in London' when you really do live in London (fingers stay together). When a statement is true, the fingers stay together, when a statement is untrue, they come apart.

- Take the attitude 'I wonder what my fingers are going to do now' rather than worrying whether you are doing it all on purpose or consciously. The reason why this exercise needs to be practised a lot is that the conscious mind often interferes in the beginning.

The next method of muscle testing I would like you to try involves a pendulum. Even though you are using a gadget to test with, you are still testing a muscle, namely a muscle in the finger that is holding the string with the pendulum. The pendulum merely functions as an extension of your finger. Good concentration is essential to make the pendulum testing work.

The pendulum exercise

This energy technique uses a pendulum as an instrument to get body biofeedback.

What to do

- Take a piece of string, about 6 inches long, and tie a ring on the end of it.

- Tie the other end of the string around your right index finger.

- Sitting at a table, firmly rest both elbows on the tabletop and support the right wrist with your left hand.

- Lower your right index finger to allow the ring to rest on the table, then gently and slowly lift the index finger so that the ring hangs freely an inch above the table top.

- Fix your gaze on the ring and keep thinking 'yes'. *Do not move your hands!* Watch what sort of movement the ring starts making. It could be either a circle, clockwise or anti-clockwise, or it could be a movement towards your body and away from it, or it could be a side-to-side movement from left to right. Whatever movement materialises is your 'yes' signal.

- Rest the ring on the table top again, then lift it gently off the surface and think 'no' continuously. *Do not move your hands!* Again, watch what movement your ring is now making. Obviously, the 'no' movement will be different from the 'yes' movement. The movement you are getting now is your 'no' response.

How long does it take?
Take your time. You may have to be patient until you get the hang of using the pendulum.

What's the aim?
To get a reliable 'yes' and 'no' response from the pendulum so that you can use it later to choose the right remedy or flower essence for yourself.

How do I know I'm doing it right?
Make random statements that are clearly true or false and see what your pendulum does. DO NOT MOVE YOUR HANDS! If you are getting the correct 'yes' or 'no' movements regularly, you have mastered it.

Tips

- If you find it easier, first practise making the pendulum move in the four different directions: clockwise, anticlockwise, left to right to left, away from you and towards you. Do so by imagining the movement in your mind and whilst holding your hands very still. See which movements come easiest and allocate 'yes' to these and 'no' to their opposites. To become a reliable tester, you will still need to practise by making true and false statements.

- Don't forget to breathe!

Now let's move on to see how you can use your newly acquired muscle testing skills to choose a flower essence that will help you resolve the problem you are currently working on.

About flower essences

The story of flower remedies began with Dr Edward Bach (1886–1936), a respected immunologist, pathologist and bacteriologist who came to the conclusion during his years of medical practice that you need to treat the person rather than the disease if you want to cure a patient. His understanding was that disease developed as a result of inner disharmony and negative thoughts manifesting on a physical level.

At the height of his medical career in 1930, Dr Bach left his lucrative practice and went to Wales to conduct research into the healing properties of flowers. Later that year, he wrote a short book called *Heal Thyself* with the message that physical disease results from being at odds with one's spiritual purpose. He also observed that people's personality and attitudes had an effect on their state of health, both physically and mentally.

Disease, to Dr Bach, was 'entirely the result of a conflict between our spiritual and mortal selves.' Health and happiness, he said, come from being in harmony with our nature. This means that it is of great importance that we do the work that we love above all else and in which we can be our true selves. In other words, it is important not just to look after the body and mind, but also to ensure that we follow a profession or vocation that fulfils our spiritual needs. In order to be happy, we need to find a balance between body, mind, emotions and the Soul.

Today, there are over sixty essence producers throughout Britain and Ireland, and many more internationally. Some make their essences from flowers, as Dr Bach did, others use gemstones, minerals or metals to create healing remedies. The essences all have one thing in common: they make an energy pattern that helps to counterbalance physical or emotional problems. They work equally well on humans, animals and plants, which means that there is more to them than just a placebo effect!

Flower essences are different from essential oils or homeopathic remedies. Flower essences are made by floating the flowers on water in the sunshine or sometimes in the moonshine. As we have seen earlier on, there is scientific evidence that water has a memory and is able to 'record' information from the substances it carries. This means that when you leave a flower floating in clean water, the water will record the energy pattern of the flower.

This recorded water is then stored with an equal amount of alcohol. This is called the 'mother tincture'. A few drops of this is put into a bottle of alcohol to make the 'stock essence' bottle that you can buy in shops. If you have an alcohol problem, make sure you go for essences that are not preserved in alcohol but in vegetable glycerin.

The vibrational pattern of a plant or flower resonates with our present health and emotional pattern. When we are unwell, a flower essence can complement our disturbed energy frequency to make us 'whole' again. When we choose an essence, we are looking for what our body or mind needs in order to be complete again. It is a bit like a vibrational jigsaw puzzle: our vibration might be too low because we are upset or frightened. We need a vibrational pattern that evens out our own distorted one.

When we have found the right complementary flower pattern, a positive shift happens that restores a balanced flow of life force in us. Flower essences repair, balance and stabilise our electro-magnetic field so that the immune and nervous systems can function optimally again.

Next time you go down to your local health food shop, have a look at what flower essences they have. Most shops will stock Bach Flower Essences, but you can also find others. Here is a list of the most common ones:

- Alaskan Essences

- Aloha Flower Essences

- Araretama Rainforest Essences

- Aum Himalaya Sankjeevini Essences

- Australian Bush Essences

- Australian Living Essences

- Bach Flower Essences

- Bailey Flower Essences

- Dancing Light Orchid Essences

- Findhorn Essences

- Hawaiian Endemic Essences

- Himalayan Essences

- Pacific Essences

- Perelandra Essences

Once you have practised your muscle testing and pendulum skills, you can determine which type of essence is relevant to you. There are various ways of making a choice.

Finding the right essence

If your local health food shop only has one type of flower

essence you are off the hook – the decision has been made for you! Alternatively, you can contact a mail order company that stocks all the above essences and check through their list (see Resources, page 183).

If you have a choice of two or more essences:

1. Do a visual survey. Read through the list of different essences and check whether there is anything in any of the essence names that appeals to you. Does one of the names particularly attract your attention in a positive way? Does it make you feel good to read the name? We often feel drawn to particular essences. Choose the one you feel attracted to.

2. When you are in the shop, pick up a bottle of, say, Bach Flower Essences, and hold it in your hand for about a minute. This allows your body to 'look' at the energy pattern of this particular type of essence. Put the bottle back and pick up a bottle of the other kind of essence, say, Australian Bush. Again, hold the bottle for a minute, then put it back.

   Pick up the first Bach Flower bottle, hold it against your palm with the last three fingers of your left hand and muscle test while concentrating on the thought, 'Is this the *best* type of essence for me?' If you are getting a 'no' response, put the bottle back and muscle test the Australian Bush bottle whilst thinking, 'Is this the *best* type of essence for me?'

   At this stage, it does not matter which of the Australian or Bach bottles you choose. Any of them will do as long as you think your question about the best *type* of essence very clearly. Any of them will do because all you are doing at this stage is to sort out which essence type you want to go with. Once you have selected the essence type, repeat the muscle testing to find which of them are the ones you need.

   You can now do another visual survey by reading the label of each bottle and picking one to three remedies that appeal to you. Alternatively, you can muscle test the bottles. Choose one, hold it in your hand for a minute, then muscle test, thinking 'Is this remedy the most appropriate and beneficial for me right now?' Select those remedies that you are getting a 'yes' response for.

3. Another way of choosing is to look at the list of different types of flower essence on page 152 and use your pendulum.

First of all, read through the list several times, and do so in a very concentrated way. Don't forget to breathe! Now pass your pendulum *very slowly* over the list and, stopping over every single name, think or say out loud, 'Show me the one that is best for me.' When you get to the right type of essence, your pendulum will respond with a clear movement, rather than just hang still.

You may wonder how this could possibly work. Think back of Dr Emoto's experiment with the little water vials, which formed beautiful crystals when they had a positive word written on the label. It is the same principle with your pendulum, which reacts to the vibrations of the flower essence names. So while you are passing the pendulum over the names, it picks up the vibration that is most beneficial to you, and this translates into movement.

Once you have selected the appropriate type of essence, you now need a list of all the single remedies within this group. Use the pendulum to choose up to three essences that are relevant for you at the moment. Think or say out loud, 'Show me which essence is the best for me!' and wait for a pendulum response. Remember to pass the pendulum very slowly over the list, stopping over every name. When you have established which essences are the right ones for you, you need to find out how many drops you need per day and for how many days you should take the essence.

To get you started, I will give you a selection of Bach Flower Remedies. This list is *not* complete! For a complete list of essences see the Resources section (page 183). Use your pendulum on the general list first, to find one relevant remedy for yourself, and then look up what this remedy is for. You may be surprised at the result! Here are some of the Bach Flower Remedies:

- Aspen
- Beech
- Clematis
- Crab Apple
- Gorse
- Heather
- Hornbeam
- Impatiens
- Olive
- Pine
- Star of Bethlehem
- Walnut

Which one of the remedies came up for you? Now look at the condition your remedy is used for:

Aspen	For people who are seized by sudden fears or worries for no specific reason and who are generally nervy and anxious. Aspen creates inner peace and security and a new zest for life.
Beech	For those who are constantly criticising, either others or themselves. Beech creates tolerance and a sense of compassion.
Clematis	For people who live in a world of their own with no interest in the real world, maybe because they have lost a loved one. Lack of concentration makes them accident-prone. Clematis creates interest in the world around and the awareness that the future is shaped by the present.
Crab Apple	A cleansing remedy for body and mind. For those who feel self-disgust, have a sense of uncleanliness

and obsessive tendencies. Crab Apple helps acceptance of one's own and other people's imperfections.

Gorse For extreme hopelessness and despair and people
who have given up the fight against a condition
they are suffering from, either mental or physical.
Gorse gives a sense of faith and hope and a more
positive outlook.

Heather A remedy for those who feel inundated by their
own problems and need to talk and think about
them all the time. Heather helps the sufferer to
become less self-centred and develop greater
understanding of other people's concerns.

Hornbeam For those who wake up in the morning and feel
weary, doubting that they have the ability to face
the day's work. Hornbeam reassures you that you
do have the strength and ability to cope well with
work, and the insight that you need to balance
work with play.

Impatiens For those who are stressed and easily irritated,
impatient and nervy. Impatiens helps you to be
less hasty in thought and action, to be calm and
diplomatic in difficult situations and with those
who are slow.

Olive For those who feel exhausted after a long period of
strain through personal difficulties, an intense
period of work, a long illness or looking after
someone else. Olive helps to restore strength,
vitality and interest in life.

Pine For people who are full of guilt and self-reproach,
blaming themselves for other people's mistakes.
Pine renews pleasure in living and instils a more
realistic sense of responsibility.

Star of Bethlehem For the after-effects of shock, mental or physical,
as a result of accidents, bad news, bereavement,
sudden disappointments, and so on. Star of
Bethlehem neutralises the effects of the shock.

Walnut This remedy protects against the effects of over-
sensitivity to certain ideas, atmospheres and

influences during major life changes (divorce, menopause, moving home, changing your job, giving up an addiction or breaking away from old ties and restrictions). Walnut helps you move forward and to make the necessary changes in life.

Dosage

You can either follow the instructions on the bottle, which may tell you that you need to put two drops in water and sip the water throughout the next hour, or you can tailor-make the dosage by muscle testing or using the pendulum. Often, we need much more or much less than the prescribed dosage the manufacturer specifies on the label, so don't be surprised if your testing yields a very different number of drops! Nor does it mean that you are 'iller' when your testing shows that you need more drops than it says on the bottle. More drops are not necessarily more effective than fewer.

To muscle test, stick the bottle into the waistband of your trousers of skirt to hold it near your body, and then ask 'How many drops do I need? More than one?' Now test to see whether you get a 'yes' or 'no' answer. If you get a 'no', you only need one drop. If you get a 'yes', continue asking, 'More than two drops?' and test again. Continue asking until you get a 'no', which indicates that you have arrived at the correct number of drops.

Example

'How many drops do I need? More than one?' ('yes' response), 'More than two?' ('yes' response), 'More than three?' ('yes' response), 'More than four?' ('no' response). This means that you do not need more than four drops, so four is the correct number of drops to take.

Now check how often you should take the drops per day. Ask, 'How many times a day do I take the drops? More than once?' (test), 'More than twice?' Keep testing until you get a 'no' as in the example above. You have now found the correct number of times a day that you need to take the essence.

Finally, check to see how many days you need to take the essence. Ask, 'For how many days do I need to take the essence? For more than one day?' (test), 'More than two days?' (test), and so on, until you get a 'no' response.

If you prefer to use your pendulum, tuck the essence bottle into your waistband and, having established which movement means 'yes' and which one means 'no', ask the following questions and wait for a 'no' response after each question:

'How many drops do I take? More than one? More than two?', etc.

'How many times a day do I take the essence? More than once? More than twice?' etc.

'For how many days do I take the essence? For more than one? More than two?' etc.

Ways of using essences

There are various ways in which you can use essences. I will mention the most common ones here, but do not let this restrict you!

By mouth

Essences can be taken either undiluted under the tongue or diluted in some water. You can test which one is best for you by asking 'What is the most beneficial and appropriate way for me to take this essence? Under the tongue?' (test), 'In water?' (test). If you are getting a 'yes' for both, then choose the method that appeals to you more. Generally, if you have a delicate stomach, the diluted form might be easier. Diluting essences does not make them weaker, by the way, but it waters down the alcohol the essence is preserved in, and that will make it easier on your stomach.

If you need to take the essence under the tongue, deposit the required number of drops directly from the essence bottle. Make sure that you don't touch the inside of your mouth with the dropper. Allow the liquid to stay in your mouth for a little while before swallowing.

If your test says that you should put the drops in water, use filtered or bottled water rather than tap water. Ideally, use 'live' water. This is water that is revitalised. When water is artificially pressed into straight lines, such as in water pipes, it loses its vital force. Water will naturally flow in curves so that it can eddy and swirl, taking oxygen in from the air which helps purify it. When water is pressed into pipes, it can no longer follow its natural movements. There are some simple devices that can restore the water's energy (see Resources, page 183).

In a bath

Essences can be soothing and healing when used in bathwater. Test how many drops you need in your bath, then run a bath but make sure that the water is not too hot. Add the required number of drops to the bathwater and swirl the water in a figure of eight to activate the essence in the water. Alternatively, you can just bathe your hands or feet in water that has been treated with the essence.

In moisturising cream

You can add a few drops of essence to your face or body moisturising cream. Put a small amount of cream in your hands, add the essence and mix it in your hands before applying it to your face or body. If you have a lotion, add the drops to the bottle and shake it well before use.

As a spray

I always spray my consulting room with water that contains a few drops of rainbow essence after each client. This clears the air and leaves the room smelling fresh and clean. You can also spray the inside of your car, your bedroom or your office – the possibilities are endless. A little essence added to a spray or watering can will also benefit ailing plants.

When you are selecting essences, don't go overboard. Stick to a maximum of three different essences and take them as long as your testing has told you to. Once you have finished them, see how you feel. Always give yourself a break of a couple of weeks before taking any other essences. The body needs time to 'process' the energy information coming from the essences.

Note also that the essences are not meant to replace any medication you are on at the moment. They will, however, enhance your physical and emotional well-being by boosting your subtle energy levels.

Rebooting your head – electro-magnetic balance

We are surrounded today by a myriad of electrical appliances and artificial electro-magnetic fields (EMFs). Within just one century, our electro-magnetic environment has changed drastically. Until the late 19th century, people still ate their supper by candlelight or kerosene lamp. In 1893, the Chicago World Fair was illuminated by Nikola Tesla's alternating-current power system, followed in 1901 by the first radiotelegraph message across the Atlantic. In 1915, the first voice transmission by radio was achieved, and with World War II came the deployment of shorter and shorter radio waves. In 1947, Bell Telephone set up the first microwave phone relay towers between New York and Boston.

Today, we are surrounded by gadgets that all run on or use electricity. The important thing to understand here is that *everything that runs on a battery or is plugged into a socket produces a magnetic field*. The human species has changed its electro-magnetic background more than any other aspect of the environment, and this is having detrimental effects on both our physical and our mental health. However, there is a lot we can do to help our body and mind cope with the artificial frequencies that surround us.

You will remember from an earlier chapter that our brains are designed to work most efficiently when we vibrate at the Earth's magnetic field frequency (see page 19). As we are surrounded by artificial frequencies, we need to take positive action to counterbalance any disturbances. Our meridian energy system is prone to be thrown out of balance when there is too much electro-smog around us.

More about EMFs

All electrical appliances emit electro-magnetic fields (EMFs). Some give off levels higher than those found under the most powerful overhead transmission lines. In experiments, digital clocks have been shown to emit a field of 6 milligauss, but emissions from many appliances produce greater counts. A computer screen can emit 20 milligauss, and a mobile phone up to 100. Typical safety limits are between 0.5 and 2, so, in theory, anything above this is unsafe.

Jean Philips of Powerwatch, an organisation which conducts research into the effects of EMF radiation, says, 'Many scientists believe the electro-magnetic sea we are bathed in, due to our use of electricity, may be damaging to our health. It can reduce our immune system's ability to fight off disease and can promote illnesses such as cancer, depression and Alzheimer's. But as long as you keep a reasonable distance from electrical equipment and think carefully about how you use it, you will be safe.'

Magnetic healing

Magnetism affects the body in a number of different ways. By wearing magnetic insoles or magnetic bracelets, you can help your body function better in the presence of electro-smog.

It is known that magnets affect the fluids in the body – that is the blood and lymph – by increasing circulation, thereby ensuring a more effective distribution of food, energy and oxygen. This, in turn, helps eliminate toxins far more efficiently. Imagine that blood cells under normal circumstances march along the blood vessels like soldiers, eyes straight ahead, backs straight, in formation. When you create a magnetic field by wearing magnetic insoles or a magnetic bracelet, the cells start to rotate on their way along the blood vessel, and this rotation allows them to pick up and release food, oxygen and hormones more effectively.

A weak electric current is generated when a magnet touches the human body, increasing the number of ions in the blood.

The pH balance of the body fluids is stabilised, and waste products and toxins are removed, bringing down cholesterol and blood pressure levels. In addition, general energy levels are increased.

There are two ways of using magnets.

Bipolar magnets

These have both negative and positive pole particles on each side. In order to combat electro-smog, bipolar magnetic insoles are a good option. You simply slip them in your shoes and wear them throughout the day or even just for a few hours in the evening. Bipolar magnets help build up the body's immune system and improve blood and lymph circulation.

Unipolar magnets

These only have one particular pole on each side.

The positive pole:

- Decreases the production of insulin.

- Strengthens weak muscles.

- Promotes tissue growth.

- Increases calcium (helpful in healing broken bones).

The negative pole:

- Arrests infections.

- Alleviates pain.

- Increases resistance to infection and disease.

- Decreases calcium build-up in joints (helpful in arthritis).

- Helps to dissolve kidney stones.

With unipolar magnets, it is important to get it right! If you are in any doubt, see a kinesiologist to find out which strength of magnet you need to use and which pole should be turned towards the body.

Electro-smog experiment

There has been a lot in the media about the potential health hazards of mobile phones, with some scientists warning against them and others ridiculing the mere notion that the radiation from mobiles could do any damage. If you yourself are not sure whether mobile phones are a risk or not, carry out the following experiment.

What to do

- Ask a friend to stretch one arm out to the side, at shoulder height.

- Switch on your mobile phone and hold it as far away from your friend's head as you can. Put your other hand on your friend's outstretched wrist.

- Exert very gentle pressure downwards whilst slowly bringing the mobile phone closer to your friend's head. Notice how close you can bring the mobile phone to your friend's head before their arm becomes weak.

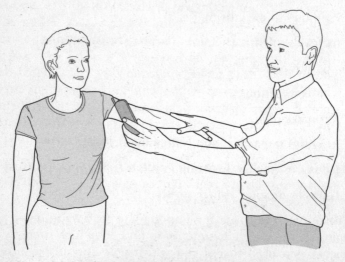

*The positions of the hands for the
electro-smog experiment.*

Most people's arm muscle goes weak when the phone is still 3 feet away from their head! This clearly shows that the body reacts with stress as the radiation waves from the phone are brought closer. Luckily, there are now a number of small devices available that can be attached to the phone and help neutralise the noxious effects (see Resources, page 183). These are small rings or plaques that have to be attached to the aerial itself or to a place near the aerial. They convert the noxious waves into brain compatible ones.

Here are a number of tips that will help you return your body and mind to its natural electro-magnetic balance.

Tips

1. Whenever possible, walk barefoot on grass. This gets your body into direct contact with the Earth's magnetic field.

2. Take showers rather than baths. The running water on and around your body clears electro-magnetic pollution and has a rebalancing effect on the body, at least temporarily. *And* you are wasting less water!

3. Another way of getting rid of electro-smog is to degauss your body. Switch your hairdryer to a cool setting and pass the motor end close by your body, starting at your head and going all the way down to your feet. Sweep down from head to toe all around the body. Hold the hairdryer sideways to avoid sucking in any hair. The alternating electro-magnetic field produced by the motor helps to diminish the effects of electro-smog temporarily. **Note: Do not degauss if you have a heart pacemaker!**

4. Place a bowl of hypertonic water in the room. Add two teaspoons of salt to each pint of water. This helps to clear the atmosphere of the room.

5. Cacti with long spikes are particularly good plants to keep in an environment where there are lots of electrical gadgets. Tests carried out by the Geophysical Laboratory of the Institut de Recherches en Géobiologie in

Switzerland have found that the species *Cereus peruvianus* is particularly effective in its ability to restore an electromagnetically disturbed environment to near normality by absorbing the radiation. It is not clear why this should be so, but one theory suggests that the very large number of long spikes on the cactus may be acting as antennae which pick up the emissions. Put a cactus in your office or your study at home, close to your computer, TV set or other equipment. If you have young children or pets, make sure your cactus is well out of reach!

6. Make sure you sleep well away from an electric or battery operated alarm clock. Keep a distance of about 6 feet if at all possible, but at least 3 feet is a must. Turn off TV sets or other electrical equipment in your bedroom before you go to sleep. Leaving them in stand-by mode is not good enough! Ideally, unplug them altogether before you go to sleep or, better still, don't have a TV set in your bedroom at all.

7. Sit at least 6 feet away from your TV set. Colour TVs give off higher EMFs than black-and-white sets.

8. If you are a heavy computer user or work in an environment with lots of electrical equipment, invest in a Teslar watch. This watch is equipped with a special chip that shields the body from the harmful effects of electricity (see Resources, page 183).

9. Washing machines and tumble dryers give off high EMFs. Ideally, let the machines run at night when you are not around, or at least leave the room while they are running.

10. Vacuum cleaners that run over the floor with an attached suction hose are safer than upright cleaners because the motor and wires are further away from you. Hand-held small vacuum cleaners are the worst because they produce high fields next to your body.

11. Electric kettles, both traditional and jug-type, create high EMFs. Heating water using electricity can change the

water's molecular structure. Some people may react badly to this change and can suffer headaches, eye problems or tremors as a consequence. Neutralise the effect by standing the mug or cup on a strong magnet while pouring the water into it. (For magnets, see Resources, page 183).

12. Underwired bras are bad news. They can act as antennae, reradiating external EMFs, including microwave frequencies, into the body. Given the increased rate of breast cancer and the genetic predisposition of some women to developing the disease, it may be better to wear bras that don't have wire in them. Some bras have plastic reinforcement, or you can simply cut a very small hole into the inside of the tube holding the wiring and pull it out. The double-stitched tubing will still give you quite a lot of support, even without the wire.

13. Radiation from microwave ovens can leak through the glass door and from around the door seals. Check your oven annually for microwave leakage, and never stand closer than 3 feet from the oven when it is on. Also, leave food to stand for at least three minutes before eating it, to allow the free radicals created in the heating process to be reabsorbed. Ideally, don't use the microwave or don't buy one in the first place. The radiation kills just about anything that is nutritious in the food.

14. Electric blankets create a magnetic field that penetrates about 6 inches into your body. They can also increase the incidence of miscarriage in women. Studies have shown that children who are exposed to even low levels of EMFs risk depression of their immune system. Use hot water bottles instead!

Counteracting geopathic stress

It is beyond the scope of this book to give a comprehensive description of geopathic stress, but as the subject is extremely important in relation to psychological and physical health, I want to include it here, albeit only briefly.

You will remember from a previous section that disturbances in the Earth's electro-magnetic field can happen in various ways. The Earth's natural and health-giving magnetic field can be disrupted by man-made underground structures such as transport tunnelling systems, or by natural phenomena such as underground rivers. Running water under pressure or in hollows in the rock structure causes a decrease in the natural geomagnetic intensity, and this can affect us adversely. Similarly, if two underground streams cross, there will be a geopathic disturbance over the crossing point.

In addition, there are also the Hartmann and Curry lines, electro-magnetically charged grids which criss-cross the Earth's surface. The grid lines are charged alternately positive and negative, and where gridlines intersect with similar charges, for example negative with negative, there is strong geopathic disturbance. At full moon, these disturbances increase.

Geopathic stress is stronger at night time when body resistance is weakest, so it is important to make sure that you do not sleep over the crossing lines of underground streams or Hartmann and Curry lines. In this respect, it does not matter whether you live on the ground floor or in the penthouse of a tower block – the negative influence of the geopathic stress in the ground under the building will still affect you.

There is insufficient evidence to prove that geopathic stress is the direct cause of diseases such as cancers, multiple sclerosis and arthritis. However, it is noticeable that the incidence of these illnesses often shows a geographically localised pattern; in other words there is a much higher than average number of people who develop a particular grave illness in that area.

It appears that geopathic stress depletes the body's energy, making a person more susceptible to an illness. Its distorting effect on the healthy electro-magnetic field of the human body leads to an imbalance. Consequently, the body is prevented from regulating itself and maintaining physiological well-being. This does not just affect physical health but also emotional well-being.

Dr Anthony Scott-Morley of the Institute of Bioenergetic Medicine reported a case of a 52-year-old man who presented with lower back pain which eventually spread to all the joints of his body. He was prescribed painkillers, but the doctors were unable to find any satisfactory explanation for the pain. The patient told Dr Scott-Morley that his personality had changed. He had become irritable and got into bad tempers for no apparent reason and had consequently lost friends. He also felt that his erratic moods had contributed to his wife asking for a divorce. Despite adequate sleep, he felt constantly tired.

The patient was advised to move his bed to a different position, and after two weeks, he reported that the pain had abated to such an extent that he could get through the day without taking pain killers. The remaining pains in his neck, shoulders and knee joints were found to be caused by the position of his desk at work where he was monitoring close circuit television all night long. He was advised to move the desk and increase the distance from the monitor. After a further two weeks, the patient reported that all the pain had gone; he felt revitalised again and was much more cheerful.

Detecting geopathic stress

The first step is to establish whether you display any of the symptoms described in the following questionnaire. Even though these symptoms may be associated with other triggers such as psychological problems, radiation, food additives or pollution, it makes sense to check whether they could result from geopathic stress.

Test for geopathic stress

1. Are you suffering from a chronic or severe illness?

2. Has this illness started or become worse since you moved to your present home?

3. Do you suffer from mood swings or irritability without any apparent reason?

4. Are you constantly tired?

5. Do you feel generally unwell without being able to put your finger on any specific symptom?

6. Is your sleep disturbed, or do you find it difficult getting to sleep?

7. Do you dream excessively?

8. Do you sleep very heavily but wake up unrefreshed?

9. Do you need an excessive amount of sleep?

10. Do you have cold feet and legs in bed?

11. Do you suffer from restless legs at night?

12. Do you suffer breathing difficulties or asthma at night?

13. Do you feel depressed?

14. Have any of the symptoms covered in 3 to 13 started or become worse since you moved to your current home?

15. Do you find yourself sleeping on the edge of the bed or curled up in a corner of the bed? (This can be a sign that you are instinctively trying to get away from the stressed area.)

16. Do you sleepwalk?

17. Have you been treated for a medical condition without getting the desired or expected results?

18. Do you keep getting relapses even though you seem to have been recovering from an illness for a while?

19. Does your cat like to sleep on your bed? (Cats seek out geopathic stress, dogs avoid it.)

20. Are many of your neighbours severely ill? (This may indicate that you live in a geographic area which has high geopathic stress levels.)

Any of these can be signs of geopathic disturbance in the ground under your bed or on the plot of land your house stands on. It does not matter how far away from the ground your bed is – geopathic disturbance will still have an effect if you live on the 50th floor of a high-rise block.

Exercise in making the right moves

Here is a simple way of checking whether you are on a grid or water intersection that saps your energy: *move your bed*!

What to do
Move your bed a few feet in one direction. If the stress is very localised, this will often be enough to remove you from the influence of the geopathic stress.

How long does it take?
Sleep in this new location for three weeks and check how you are feeling emotionally and physically.

What's the aim?
To test whether there is geopathic stress where the bed stood originally. To move away from that stress so you can recover emotionally and physically.

Troubleshooting
After three weeks of sleeping in the new position, I still have the same symptoms. Move the bed again. Move it a further few feet away.

I've had my bed in every conceivable position in my bedroom and it hasn't made a blind bit of difference! Make sure you are not committing any electro-magnetic 'sins' by, for example, having your alarm clock near your head while you are sleeping (see page 162). Also consider that the geopathic problem might originate from your workplace. Your desk may be in the wrong position. Shift the desk if your boss will let you. If nothing yields any results, you can employ a professional dowser who will check your property. A dowser who specialises in geopathic stress will also be able to remedy the faulty geopathic flux. Today, many dowsers can do the checking by dowsing over a map of the area where you live and by dowsing the floorplan of your house. For contact details, see Resources (page 183).

Surfing everyday chaos

You can be healthy and happy, but still suffer from the stresses of everyday living. This section is about keeping sane and in balance even if everything else around you is chaotic.

With the best will in the world, we cannot *make* life run smoothly all the time, so sometimes all we can do is go for damage limitation. Remember, however, that having a lot to do is not the same thing as being stressed. Just like beauty, stress is in the eye of the beholder!

Once you have worked through the exercises in this book, you will notice your stress levels come down considerably. Things that used to upset you in the past just make you shrug your shoulders now, and what you considered a nuisance, an imposition or an injustice before, you can now deal with in a calm and efficient manner. This new-found inner balance and confidence will help to make you feel more centred and strong.

The following quick and easy exercises provide an excellent 'maintenance' programme to keep your Self together. They are also very good first aid for resetting the brain, body and emotions to their positive default settings, so it is worth spending a little time learning to do them properly.

The first exercise, the thymus tap, comes from kinesiology. We use it as a quick balancing mechanism for the body, and you may want to do it before you start muscle testing with fingers or the pendulum.

The next exercise is very useful if you feel emotionally unsettled, and also if you have an allergic reaction to a food or a substance. If you are doing it for an allergy, you only have to tap points 1 to 4; for emotional stress, use all 5 points.

Thymus tap exercise

For thousands of years it has been known that the thymus gland is the seat of life energy. The thymus is a pyramid-shaped organ that lies immediately beneath the breastbone at the level of the heart. It is the link between body and mind and is the first organ to be affected when we are stressed.

A healthy, active thymus is essential for health as it helps the lymph system drain foreign matter, cellular debris and toxins from the cells so these can be carried to the bloodstream for disposal. Thymus hormones also activate T-cells, which are vitally important in immunological surveillance and directly concerned with resistance to infections and cancer. When you are stressed through overwork, anxiety, depression, trauma or any other circumstances or illnesses, the thymus contracts and cannot work efficiently.

What to do

Tap lightly but firmly around the thymus area as indicated in the illustration below. Tap in an anticlockwise circle. You should complete the circle in about ten taps.

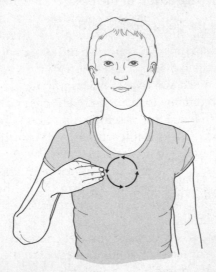

Where to tap in the thymus tap exercise.

How long does it take?

Tap about six to eight times around the thymus.

What's the aim?

To stimulate the thymus. To rebalance and harmonise the body's energy system.

Together with the zip up (see page 138), the thymus tap is a good way of waking the body up in the morning. If you need to unwind during the day or in the evening, the thymus tap can be used again, but in addition, also use the stress tap. This is how you do it.

Stress tap exercise

The stress tap is an abbreviated version of the emotions tap. Use it whenever you feel stressed through overwork, worrying or illness.

What to do

Tap firmly, between five and ten times, on the following points (see illustration, page 89):

1. Eyebrows (at the point closest to the nose).

2. Under eyes.

3. Under arms.

4. Collarbones.

5. Side of one hand.

How long does it take?

Do three rounds of tapping, then check whether you feel better and more relaxed. If not, do another three rounds of the same tapping sequence.

What's the aim?

To allow the body to let go of stress. To be able to think more clearly and feel more 'together' again.

Sometimes, it can also be useful to balance out any lop-sidedness that may arise through doing a lot of intellectual work or through being very emotional. If you are stressed by over-thinking or over-feeling, one side of your brain becomes overworked.

Cross crawl exercise

The brain consists of two halves: the left and the right hemispheres. The left side of the brain controls the right side of the body and the right side controls the left side of the body.

There is also a separation in the functions of the brain. The left hemisphere carries out tasks that require analytical, logical thinking, and it works in a linear fashion. This means that it allows us to look at events in sequential order. The right hemisphere, on the other hand, is involved in emotional aspects and creative activities, where mental connections are made that are omni-directional and holistic rather than linear.

When we are out of balance or no longer feel ourselves, the following cross crawl exercises help the brain even out any over-use of one particular hemisphere. You may have had to do a lot of thinking and analysing during the day, so that the left hemisphere of your brain is overworked. Or you may be going through an emotional crisis because things in your private or professional life are all going wrong for you, in which case the right hemisphere has been over-used. With the cross crawl exercises, you help to integrate the left and right hemispheres, improve concentration, move lymph around and reduce stress. Use the illustrations on pages 172–3 to help you understand the following exercises.

What to do

1. March on the spot with exaggerated knee and arm movements.

2. Swing your right arm far forwards while stretching the right leg backwards, then push the left arm forwards with the left leg going backwards.

3. Raise your right knee up and touch it with your left elbow. Raise your left knee up and touch it with your right elbow.

4. Raise your left arm in the air and stretch your right leg sideways away from the body. Raise your right arm up in the air and stretch your left leg sideways away from the body.

5. Raise your left arm in the air and stretch out your left leg sideways. Raise your right arm in the air and stretch your right leg sideways away from the body.

Step 1

Step 2

Step 3

Step 4   *Step 5*

How long does it take?
Do each cross crawl sequence twenty times.

What's the aim?
To reduce emotional and physical stress. To enhance coordination. To feel more focused and energised.

Knowing when you are whole again

It can be amazingly easy to overlook signs that you are getting better. People expect progress to happen in a spectacular and very visible manner, and when it happens quietly and unobtrusively, they cannot see or recognise it. It's a bit like looking for a letterbox in a foreign country. In England, letterboxes are red, so when you want to post a letter in Germany, you may be unable to find one because you are looking for something red when letterboxes in Germany are yellow. I am convinced that half the problem in life for many people is that they do not recognise when they are successful. Let me explain.

Many years ago, I had a client at my hypnotherapy practice who came to see me for a fear of eating in public. He loathed having to go out with family or friends, he made every excuse under the sun to refuse invitations, and he had successfully avoided restaurants for the last year. On a rational level, he could see it was silly and that he was depriving himself of one of life's pleasures, but on an emotional level, he felt so afraid that he was unable to eat out.

We worked through some issues in his past which were connected with his phobia, and after four sessions, I expected to see some progress, so when he came in for his next appointment, I asked him how he was doing with his problem and he replied, 'Still the same.' As this is not an answer we therapists like to hear, I decided to dig a bit deeper and asked, 'So you haven't been eating out over the last week?' He thought for a moment and, with a puzzled look on his face, said yes, he had actually eaten out.

It turned out that not only had he accepted an invitation, but when he got to the venue early, instead of waiting outside for the others as he would have done in the bad old days, he had also calmly walked inside and had a drink at the bar. Soon his friends arrived and they all had a very nice meal and a pleasant evening together.

So why did my client tell me initially that his problem hadn't changed? The answer is that he didn't notice. Maybe he expected it to be a long time before he could see progress, and so he didn't look out for it. It all went so easily and effortlessly: accepting the invitation, going to the restaurant, eating and having a nice time – it just didn't seem to be anything special. No trumpet sounds, no big sign in the sky that said,

'Congratulations! You've done it!' Instead, he just went and did it and it was no big deal.

On that day, I learnt something important, and that is not to take 'no' for an answer when I ask a client whether they have noticed any positive changes since their last session. Invariably, the client has made some progress somewhere along the line but is unaware of it. He is looking for a red letterbox in a country of yellow letterboxes.

An easy way of discovering whether you are making progress on your journey of personal development is to go back to your tests in Chapter 3. You were asked to evaluate whether you were trapped in a negative life pattern (see page 73), whether the past still had a hold on you (see page 84) and whether negative thoughtforms were blocking you (see page 98). Since then, provided you have been practising the various exercises, you will have actively effected some shifts in perception, and this always results in some form of progress. But are you aware of that progress?

Progress check

- Go through the tests on pages 73, 84 and 98 and grade your reactions to each statement in the way that you did before.

- Compare the answers you are giving this time with those you gave when you did the tests the first time around.

You will notice that some of the statements apply less than they did – you have given them a lower grading than the first time. This, clearly, means that you are making progress.

If you have not made any progress, then you either have not done any of the exercises or you have not done them often enough. This book is really good, you know, but only if you pull your finger out and *do* the exercises!

When you take positive action, not only will your thoughts change and the way you view past experiences, but your circumstances and environment will reflect the inner progress you are making. A very good friend of mine had been having great problems with her ageing mother who was demanding, often unreasonable and at times downright rude.

When my friend changed her attitude and became more confident, it also changed the way she related to her mother. She was no longer hesitant and diffident with her mother, but instead became firmer and bolder, although she always stayed kind and understanding.

The effects on her mother were amazing: she became less difficult and more respectful towards her daughter. By working on herself, my friend had not only made herself feel better, but she had also positively influenced her mother's behaviour. This enabled her to go on loving her mother and to continue looking after her happily rather than grudgingly.

So why do we so often not recognise our own success? I think part of the problem is that many aims we have in life can only be achieved over a period of time.

Say you want to lose weight. Your aim is to go down from 11 stone to 9 stone and so far, you have lost 2 pounds. It is understandable that you are looking at your 9-stone target and feel a bit daunted because you still have so far to go.

Similarly, you may want to become more confident in work meetings. So far, all you have done is answer one question someone asked you during the last meeting, but what you really want to be able to do is to participate more actively, speak freely and feel calm and relaxed doing so. You have not achieved either goal – weight loss or self-assertion – in fact, you have only moved a little way towards your aim at this point in time.

You now have two choices: you can either have a whingefest about how far you still have to go and how difficult it will be to reach your goal, or you can feel pleased and proud of yourself for the progress you have made. Basically, you are making a choice between being appreciative of your own efforts and therefore happy, or ignoring your progress and being unhappy. I know which one I would rather go for.

It is very important to set goals in life: there is no doubt about that. If you have no aim, you can't get lost, but you will also never arrive. But when you set an aim for yourself, it is also important to look at and be aware of intermediate steps that will tell you that you are progressing. After all, when your baby takes its first steps and still falls down ten times on its way across the room, you wouldn't dream of kicking it and saying, 'You have wasted nine months of my life!' You know that this small progress is valuable and will eventually lead to smooth and confident walking, running and jumping. So why not treat yourself as happily and hopefully as you would your toddler?

Look at any progress you make in whatever you do, congratulate yourself from the bottom of your heart and let this happiness help to propel you further forward on your way towards making your dreams come true.

Feeling whole again comes when you have confronted your demons, even if you are still struggling with them at times. Being in touch with your Self is the first step to becoming whole and feeling intact again. As you can imagine, being whole is a very subjective experience, so ultimately, you are the only person who can assess whether you have actually achieved this or not.

Here are a few points that show you that you are succeeding:

- You feel you have control over a great number of things in your life and, where you don't, accept this calmly.

- Your life situation is difficult, but you have clear plans to resolve the problems and confidently go about implementing the necessary changes.

- You feel more peaceful inside and can allow other people to be as they want to be.

- You can sit still without doing anything and feel calm and content.

- Your health is improving.

- Your energy levels are improving.

- You can let go of people who are detrimental to your well-being.

- You stop feeling driven to do things.

- You can view the past with greater detachment.

- You laugh and smile more.

- Little things can make you happy.

- You feel you have a special place in this world.

- You feel you are important and that you count.

In the end, only you can say that you are whole again. As long as you keep looking for positive solutions, as long as you keep an open mind about the way the solutions present themselves, and as long as you don't give up, you will succeed. It may take a while and it may be hard, but it can be done. Don't believe in miracles – rely on them. They happen every day, and just like everyone else, you can make them happen for yourself.

Further Reading

Arthur Bailey, *Anyone Can Dowse for Better Health*, Quantum, 1999.
The title says it all! Easy-to-learn techniques to help yourself with dowsing.

Robert O. Becker and Gary Selden, *The Body Electric – Electromagnetism and the Foundation of Life*, Quill, 1985.
One of the best books about the biological effects of magnetic fields on health and healing, written by a pioneering researcher.

Roger J. Callahan with Richard Turbo, *Tapping the Healer Within. Using Thought Field Therapy to instantly conquer fears, anxieties and emotional distress*, Piatkus, 2001.
Easy-to-follow steps show you how to tap energy points on the body to treat phobias, compulsions, trauma, anxiety, depression and physical pain.

Miranda Castro, *The Complete Homeopathy Handbook. A guide to everyday health care*, Macmillan, 1990.
An excellent comprehensive guide that describes the principles of homeopathy and lists the most commonly used remedies, along with a repertory of illnesses they can be used for. It gives clear advice about how you can safely use homeopathic remedies if you want to treat yourself or your family.

Donna Eden, *Energy Medicine*, Piatkus, 1998.
The definitive book on how to use your body's energies for optimum health and vitality. Contains many energy exercises for both emotional and physical problems you may want to tackle. Excellent illustrations show you where the meridians run, and clear explanations are given about how the body's energy system works. If you buy any of the books mentioned here, buy this one!

Masaru Emoto, *Messages from Water*, Hado Kyoikusha, 1999.
A beautiful book with excellent colour photographs of water crystals before and after they have been prayed over or treated with positive thought. Descriptions of various experiments that have been carried out with water to show that it is indeed carrying messages.
Order online at www.hado.com

Richard Gerber, *Vibrational Medicine for the 21st Century*, Piatkus, 2000.
An excellent book written by a medical doctor who presents the latest scientific research about the power of thought and consciousness, as well as subtle energies. A user-friendly guide to key therapies including homeopathy, acupuncture, flower essences, colour and light therapy, magnet therapy and radionics.

Judy Howard, *The Bach Flower Remedies Step by Step*, C.W. Daniel, 1990.
A complete practical guide to choosing and using the remedies. It contains full descriptions of each remedy and includes detailed advice on selecting remedies, recognising type remedies, treating animals and plants, and the preparation and administration of the remedies.

Liz Koch, *The Psoas Book*, Greensleeves Books, Oxford.
A comprehensive guide to the location, function and effect of the psoas muscle. Contains easy-to-do exercises to relax and strengthen the psoas.
Order online at www.guineapigpub.com

Ilana Kronberger and Siegbert Lattacher, *On The Track of Water's Secret, From Victor Schauberger to Johann Grander*, Uranus, 1995.
This book shows that water has a memory and that it is capable of transferring information through particle oscillation, which means that ecologically dead rivers and lakes can be revived. It also presents the case that energised water has a positive effect on human beings, animals and plants, with a wealth of case histories.

Maggie La Tourelle with Anthea Courtenay, *Thorson's Principles of Kinesiology*, Thorsons, 1997.
A good general guide to different types of kinesiology, its history, application areas and self-help techniques. Full of very encouraging case histories of people who have benefited from this wonderful therapy.

Gary Null, *Healing with Magnets*, Robinson, 1998.
A good basic guide on magnet therapy, clinicians' reports and scientific research into the healing power of magnets.

Vera Peiffer, *Positive Living*, Piatkus, 2001.
Effective strategies for dealing creatively with every aspect of your life, from work and health to relationships and emotional problems. Includes an A–Z of common problems with advice, affirmations and visualisations to help overcome each one.

Vera Peiffer, *Positive Thinking. Everything you have always known but were afraid to put into practice.* Thorsons, 2001.
A fun and easy-to-read guide to why and how positive thinking works. The book introduces easy-to-learn techniques and teaches you how to apply them successfully in everyday life. Lots of practical advice as well as scripts and affirmations.

Vera Peiffer, *Positively Fearless*, Thorsons, 2001.
This book explains how fear can develop and what different types of fear exist, and introduces a fear scale that allows you to measure how strong your fears are. A great number of exercises help you to overcome your fear.

Jane Thurnell-Read, *Geopathic Stress, How earth energies affect our lives*. Element, 1995.
An excellent introduction to the topic. The book explains clearly the symptoms of geopathic stress, its different types, how to detect and correct it.

Ian White, *Australian Bush Flower Essences*, Findhorn Press, 1999.
Ian White is the leading expert on Australian Bush Flower Essences. In this book, he describes each flower individually, giving clear descriptions of how to use it.

Resources

Environmental protection agencies

Friends of the Earth
Established in the UK in 1971, now the largest international green organisation. Campaigns against threats such as climate change, pollution and modified foods.
Information: 020 7490 1555
Donations: 0800 581 051
www.foe.co.uk

Greenpeace
A global organisation with offices in more than 30 countries. Campaigns to protect the environment and actively works to prevent whaling and the dumping of radioactive waste into the oceans.
Information: 020 7865 8100
www.greenpeace.org.uk

WWF – The Global Environment Network
An international organisation with almost five million supporters in 96 countries. Protects endangered species and addresses global threats to nature such as climate change.
Information: 01483 426 444
www.wwf.org.uk

Geopathic stress and electro-magnetic field disturbances

Atmosphere Technologies Ltd.
Global House
Ashley Road
Epsom
Surrey KT18 5AD

For a Cell-Plus device for your mobile phone to protect you from noxious effects:
Tel. 0844 884 1966
www.cellplus.co.uk

British Society of Dowsers
2 St Ann's Road
Malvern
Worcestershire
WR14 4RG
01684 576 969
www.britishdowsers.org

If you need help from a professional dowser to determine whether you have geopathic stress problems at home or at work, contact the society for practitioners who can help.

Powerwatch
Offers the latest information pertaining to electro-magnetic field disturbances in the home.
www.powerwatch.org.uk

Magnets

Tools for Energy, Balance and Health
25 Hainthorpe Road
London SE27 0PL
Order line: 0845 658 0012
www.toolsforenergy.com

Magnetic insoles, magnetic bracelets, bioelectric shields against EMF radiation, Teslar watches, strong magnet rings for water purification, pendulums and much more. Ask for a catalogue.

Energised water

Ultimate Water Ltd.
1 Mayfield Avenue
London W4 1PN
Tel. 08701 780 800
www.grander.co.uk

Distributors of energised water devices for the house and handbag. Ask for a catalogue.

Flower essences

The Nutri Centre
Unit 3
Kendal Court
Kendal Avenue
London W3 0RU
For a list of their flower essences, ask for their full catalogue. Nutri Centre stock all the flower essences mentioned on page 152 and supply by mail order.
Information and order hotline: 0845 602 2188
www.nutricentre.com

The Dr Edward Bach Centre
Mount Vernon
Baker's Lane
Brightwell-cum-Sotwell
Oxon OX10 0PZ
Tel. 01491 834678
www.bachcentre.com

Contact the centre for books by and about Edward Bach. The centre also arranges courses and sells the Bach Flower essences.

Natural therapies

Acupuncture
Acupuncture involves the stimulation of acupuncture points with very fine needles in order to help the gland or organ that is connected with that acupuncture point.

British Acupuncture Council
63 Jeddo Road
London W12 9HQ
Tel. 020 8735 0400
Fax 020 8735 0404
www.acupuncture.org.uk

Healing
The healer acts as a channel for subtle energy or spiritual healing forces which help alleviate physical and emotional problems.

National Federation of Spiritual Healers
Old Manor Farm Studio
Church Street
Sunbury-on-Thames
Middlesex TW16 6RG
Tel. 01932 783164
www.nfsh.org.uk

Health Kinesiology
An indicator muscle is tested to identify stresses on the individual's energy system. Acupuncture points are held to bring the body back into balance.

Health Kinesiology UK
www.hk4health.co.uk

Herbalism

An ancient worldwide system of medicine using plants to prevent and cure disease.

The National Institute of Medical Herbalists
Elm House
54 Mary Arches Street
Exeter EX4 3BA
Tel. 01392 426022
Fax 01392 498963
www.nimh.org.uk

Homeopathy

Homeopathy is governed by the principle that agents which produce certain symptoms in health also cure those symptoms in disease, and that the more a drug is diluted, the more powerful it becomes.

Society of Homoeopaths
11 Brookfield
Duncan Close
Moulton Park
Northampton
NN3 6WL
Tel. 0845 450 6622
Fax 0845 450 6622
www.homoeopathy-soh.uk.org

Hypnotherapy

A very well-established and effective method of helping with depressive illnesses, using the hypnotic state to work through traumatic events to gain or regain confidence and self-esteem.

Corporation of Advanced Hypnotherapy
Tel. 01945 882067
www.hypno-corp.org

Psychotherapy

The National Council of Psychotherapists was established in 1971 and offers a register of qualified members who work with different types of psychotherapy. The NCP also provides further training for practitioners.

National Council of Psychotherapists (NCP)
P.O. Box 7219
Heanor
DE75 9AG
Tel. 0845 230 6072
www.ncphq.co.uk

Reflexology

An ancient Chinese and Indian diagnostic and therapeutic system in which the soles of the feet and sometimes the palms of the hands are massaged.

The British Reflexology Association
Monks Orchard
Whitbourne
Worcester WR6 5RB
Tel. 01886 821207
Fax 01886 821017
www.britreflex.co.uk

Reiki

Reiki is a form of healing whereby the practitioner channels energy through their hands on to the person they are treating.

The Reiki Association
Westgate Court
Spittal
Haverfordwest
SA62 5QP
Tel. 07704 270 727
Email. enquiries@reikiassociation.org.uk
www.reikiassociation.org.uk

Thought Field Therapy

Devised by Dr Roger Callahan, a clinical psychologist, this method helps overcome trauma, physical pain, phobias, depression and a great number of other psychological problems by tapping acupuncture points, mainly on the face and on the hands. Works very well for jetlag too!

Callahan Techniques, Ltd.
PO Box 1220
La Quinta CA 92247
Tel. 001 760 564 1925
www.tftrx.com

For courses in England, contact
Robin Ellis
Rumwood
Horseheath
Cambridge CB1 6QX
Tel. 01223 892596
robinellis@rumwood.demon.co.uk

Positive Thinking

Simple and effective strategies for everyone who wants to learn how to gain greater confidence, using visualisation, affirmations and other strategies to overcome past trauma. Correspondence course and practical training, as well as a qualification to become a Positive Thinking counsellor.

The Peiffer Foundation
PO Box 139A
Surbiton
KT6 6WE
Tel. 020 8241 1962
www.vera-peiffer.com

Index

A

acupuncture points 2, 18, 87
adolescents 72
aims 176–7
air pollution 52
alarm clocks 162
alcohol consumption
  case study of 50–1
  dependence on 63–4
  emptiness of 4
allergies
  as cause of disconnection 47–8
  dealing with 168–9
  'masked' 48
allopathic medicine 17
anger 57–9
anorexia nervosa 38
anxiety 56–7
appearance, obsession with 4
aspen 152
astronauts 21
attitudes
  conditioning of 37–9
  towards pain 47

B

Bach, Edward 147
Bach Flower Essences 149, 150, 151–2
baths 156
beech 152
belief systems, personal 33, 81–2
Bennett, Terence 135
biofeedback 15
bipolar magnets 159
blood flow 135, 158–9
body
  see also physical health
  balancing 168, 169–70
  connecting with 117–19
  mind-body connection 2, 15–17, 95
    positive visualisation for 126–8
    and the Soul 30
body image 38
bracelets, magnetic 158–9
brain 137, 139, 171
bras, underwired 163
bubble bath 49
bulimia nervosa 3, 38
Burr, Harold S. 142

C

cacti 161–2
Callaghan, Roger 87
cannabis 50
case studies
  alcohol abuse 50–1
  attitude conditioning 38–9
  changing perceptions 102–3, 105, 106–7
  detrimental relationships 39–40
  geopathic stress exposure 55–6
  feelings of incompleteness 31–2
  letting go of the past 87–8
  loneliness 60
  negative life patterns 70–2
  feelings of resentment/anger 58
  'swapping places' 106–7
  power of thought 96–7
Central Vessel (CV) 137, 138–9
change see life changes
chemical overload 20, 48–9
childhood, memories of 86
Chinese medicine 17
circulation 135, 158–9
clematis 152
coincidence 24–5
collarbone breathing exercise 87, 88–90

commuting 42
competitiveness 42
completeness
  achievement of 66–178
    being true to your Self 108–78
    clearing up the past 67,
      68–107
    introduction 67–8
  defining 8
  what make us feel? 8–30
conditioning 37–9
connectivity 4, 131–2, 139–41
continual learning 42
crab apple 152–3
cravings 48
creativity, unexpressed 44–5
critical people 115, 152
cross crawl exercise 171–3
Curry Lines 54, 164

D
day-dreamers 152
degaussing 161
dependency 63–5
depression 56–7, 58, 114–15
despair 153
detrimental relationships 39–41
disability 47
disconnection
  consequences of 56–65
  reasons for 35–56
    environmental 51–6
    physical 46–51
    psychological 35–46
divorce 31–2, 46
dowsing 26, 168
drugs, recreational
  as cause of disconnection 49–50
  dependence on 64–5
  emptiness of 4
dysfunctional families 38–9

E
Earth
  connecting with 131–2, 139–41
  electro-magnetic field of 19, 20,
    21, 26, 54
eating disorders 3, 38
eating out, phobia of 174–5
Ego 27–8
electric blankets 163
electric currents, rogue 20

electro-magnetic disturbance 20,
  51, 53–4
  balancing 157–63
    electro-smog experiment
      160–1
    magnetic healing 158–9
    tips for 161–3
electro-magnetic fields (EMFs)
  18–22, 157–8
  Earth's 19, 20, 21, 26, 54
  human 21
electro-magnetic system 18–19, 20,
  21
electro-photography 142
emotional routines 72–3
emotional stress 20
emotional withdrawal 23
emotions 9–11, 15
  assessing 10–11
  balanced 4–5, 30, 168–9, 170–1
  defining healthy 10
  intense 116
  negative 121–2, 129–30
  positive 121–2
  transforming through positive
    thought 94–102
  positive visualisation for 128–30
  suppressed 9–10
  tuning into 119–22
Emoto, Masaru 22, 110, 112, 151
emptiness 3–4
  signs of 62–3
  understanding 6–65
    introduction 7
    what makes us complete? 8–30
    why do we feel incomplete?
      31–65
energy see subtle energy
'energy patterns' 22
environment, and disconnection
  51–6
Erickson, Milton H. 82
everyday stressors 168–73
exercises
  collarbone breathing 87, 88–90
  combating geopathic stress 167–8
  connecting with your physical
    world 117–19
  cross crawl 171–3
  electro-smog experiment 160–1
  evaluating your thoughts 111–12
  finger muscle testing 143–5
  future projection 133–4

meridian tap 87, 91–3
Mother Earth and Father Sky
139–41
pendulum muscle testing 143,
145–7
positive visualisation for the body
127–8
positive visualisation for the
emotions 129–30
positive visualisation for the spirit
131–2
psoas exercise 75–80, 85
screen exercise 103–5
self-preservation reset 99–102
soothing the body and mind
136–7
spreading positive vibrations 113
stress tap 168–9, 170–1
swapping places 106–7
thymus tap 168, 169–70
tuning into your emotions
120–2
tuning into your spirit 123–5
'zipping up' 138–9
experience
impact on the Self 80–7
interpretation of 33

F
failure 36, 82
families
contact with 42, 62
dysfunctional 38–9
fatigue 153
fear
affect on the body 16
overcoming 75–6, 91–3, 96–7,
152
flashbacks 37, 86
flexibility 9
flower essences 29, 147–57
baths 156
dosages 154–5
finding the right essence 149–54
moisturisers 156
oral administration 155–6
sprays 156–7
types 149
ways of using 155–7
freelancers 62
Friends of the Earth 51
future projection exercise 132–4

G
general practitioners (GPs) 13,
49–50
geopathic stress 20, 51, 54–6
counteracting 163–8
detecting 165–8
symptoms of 54–5
gorse 153
gossip 115
Governing Vessel (GV) 137
grass, walking on 161
Greenpeace 51
guilt 86, 153

H
hairdryers 161
Hartmann Lines 54, 164
healing
magnetic 158–9
movements 134–41
process 3
heather 153
homeopathy 142
hornbeam 153
household chemicals 20, 49
hypnotherapy 15–16

I
illness
as cause of disconnection 47
chronic 86–7
as disruption in the flow of subtle
energy 13, 17, 20–1, 23, 24
as result of spiritual and mortal
conflict 147–8
imagery, mental 69
immune system 16
impatience 153
impatiens 153
incompleteness 31–65
case study of 31–2
consequences of 56–65
reasons for feeling 35–56
Independent (newspaper) 64
injury 47
inner world, tuning into 117–25
connecting with your emotions
119–22
connecting with your physical
world 117–19
connecting with your spirit
122–5

insoles, magnetic 158–9
intolerances 47–8

J
*Journal of the American Medical
    Association* 50

K
kettles 162–3
kinesiology 25, 87, 95, 168
    see also muscle testing
    defining 2
    magnetic healing 159
    prejudice regarding 142
Kirlian, Semyon 142
Kyoto Agreement 51

L
learning, continual 42
life changes 45–6, 153–4
life force 29
    see also subtle energy
life patterns, negative 69, 70–80
    case studies 70–2
    letting go of 75–80
    testing for 73–5
loneliness 35, 59–61
loss 82

M
magnetic healing 158–9
    bipolar magnets 159
    unipolar magnets 159
magnetism 19–21
    see also electro-magnetic
        disturbance; electro-magnetic
        fields; electro-magnetic system
massage 134–5
meaning, sense of 63
mechanical shock 20
medication, as cause of
        disconnection 49–50
meditation 123
memory
    see also past
    childhood 86
mental health 9, 11–12, 15
    assessing 11–12
    defining 11
    and recreational drugs 50, 65
mental imagery 69

meridian tap (exercise) 87, 91–3
meridians 17–19, 20–1, 87, 88
    blocks 137, 138
    Central Vessel 137, 138–9
    exercises for 87, 91–3, 138–9
    Governing Vessel 137
    role of 137–8
    scientific evidence for 18
    sensing 138
microwaves 163
mind-body connection 2, 15–17,
        95
mobile phones 158, 160–1
moisturisers 156
'mother tincture' 148
muscle memory 126
muscle testing 2, 25, 26, 143–7
    finger exercise 143–5
    of flower remedies 150–1, 154–5
    pendulum exercise 143, 145–7

N
nature, wisdom of 141–7
negative thought 93, 94–102
    assessing 97–9, 111–12
    power of 109–10, 111, 114–16
    protective function of 99–102
    resolving 99–102
    and social interaction 109–10,
        111–12, 114–16
neighbours 42
nervous breakdowns 31–2
nervous system 18–19, 20
neurovascular (NV) reflex points
        135
New Scientist 48
noise pollution 52

O
oestrogen 48–9
olive 153
oral contraceptives 49
over-sensitivity 153–4

P
pain, dealing with 47, 119
parental influence 33
past 33
    and attitude conditioning 37–9
    clearing up 67, 68–107
        assessing the impact of your
            past 83–7

changing your perceptions
102–7
eliminating negative life
patterns 69, 70–80
emotional transformation
94–102
letting go of the past 87–93
overcoming a limiting past
80–93
and disconnection 36–7
dwelling on 37
pendulums
for choosing flower remedies
151–2, 154, 155
muscle testing with 143, 145–7
perceptions, changing 33–4, 102–7
personal appearance, obsession with
4
personal belief systems 33, 81–2
personal energy 23–4
personal space 32–3
personality 32–3, 80, 81
Philips, Jean 158
phobias 174–5
physical health 9, 12–13, 15
see also body
assessing 12–13
as cause of disconnection 46–51
defining 12
pine 153
pollution 52
positive thought 1, 3, 15, 23,
94–102, 108
evaluating personal 111–12
exercise for 99–102
remote power of 110, 112–13
and social interaction 110–13
positive visualisation 125–32
for the body 126–8
for the emotions 128–30
for the spirit 130–2
possessions, obsession with 4
possessiveness 40
Powerwatch organisation 158
progress 174–8
checks for 175–8
psoas exercise 75–80, 85
psychological causes of
disconnection 35–46
psychotherapy 24

R
rationality 11

rejection 83
relationships
changing 46
detrimental 39–41
negative patterns in 70–2
relaxation exercises 88–90
resentment 57–9
rootlessness 61–2

S
scar tissue 20–1
Scott-Morley, Anthony 165
screen exercise 103–5
Self 8, 27, 28, 29
see also body; emotions; physical
health; spiritual health
being true to 108–78
electro-magnetic balance
157–63
everyday stress 168–73
flower essences 147–57
future projection 132–4
geopathic stress 163–8
healing movements 134–41
knowing when you are whole
again 173–8
positive visualisation 125–32
social interaction 108, 109–16
tuning into your inner world
117–25
wisdom of nature 141–7
establishing a positive sense of 80
impact of experience on 80–7
losing touch with 23, 32, 33,
34–5, 70
see also disconnection
and social interaction 28, 31, 32,
80
self-centredness 153
self-disgust 152–3
self-preservation reset exercise
99–102
shampoo 49
shock
flower remedies for 153
mechanical 20
shopping urge 4
shower gel 49
showers 161
singles 59–60
skin-to-skin contact 135
sleeping 162
social interaction 108, 109–16

sodium laureth sulphate (SLES) 49
sodium lauryl sulphate (SLS) 49
Soul 14–15, 27, 28–9, 30
sound 22
space, personal 32–3
spiritual health 9, 13–15
  positive visualisation for 130–2
  pursuit of 30
  tuning into 122–5, 139–41
sprays, flower essences 156–7
star of Bethlehem 153
'stock essence' 148
stress 20
  as cause of disconnection 41–3
  everyday 168–73
  flower remedies for 153
  signs of 43
stress tap exercise 168–9, 170–1
subtle energy 17–27, 137–8, 142–3
  blocks to 13, 17, 20–1, 23, 24,
    137, 138, 142
  illness as disruption in the flow of
    13, 17, 20–1, 23, 24
  meridians 17–19, 20–1, 87, 88,
    91–3, 137–9
  personal energy 23–4
  universal energy 24–7
suffering 34
sun screens, dangers of 48–9
'swapping places' 105–7

T
teenagers 72
Teslar watches 162
thought 69, 94–102
  evaluating personal 111–12
  negative 93–102, 109–12,
    114–16
  positive 1, 3, 15, 23, 94–102,
    108, 110–13
Thought Field Therapy 87
thoughtforms 95, 96, 97–8, 99–100
thymus tap exercise 168, 169–70

touch, healing power of 134–7
trauma 36–7, 83, 91–3
tumble dryers 162
TV 162

U
underwired bras 163
unhappiness 4
unipolar magnets 159
universal energy 24–7
universe, connecting with 131–2,
  139–41

V
vacuum cleaners 162
Vernejoul, Pierre de 18
vibration
  defining 19, 21–3
  and flower remedies 148, 151
violence 57–9
visualisation, positive 125–32
  for the body 126–8
  for the emotions 128–30
  for the spirit 130–2

W
walnut 153–4
washing machines 162
watches, Teslar 162
water
  electrical heating of 162–3
  hypertonic 161
  'live' 156
wholeness, recognition of 173–8
words, vibrations of 22–3, 151–4
workplace
  changes in 46
  and rootlessness 61, 62

Z
'zip up' exercise 138–9